ALSO BY W. SCOTT MOORE

Dead Ends or Destiny?
Seven Paths through the
Wilderness Experiences of Life

Exit Wounds:
Healing from the Hurts of the Ministry

Partners in Planting:
Starting and Staffing a New Testament Church

Rural Revival:
-Growing Churches in Shrinking Communities

Supernatural Strategy:
Discovering the Lost Key to Effective Evangelism

Uganda's Messianic Muslim:
How Jesus Christ is Transforming
the Life and Ministry of Nassan Ibrahim

FOR THE RURAL CHURCH

*The Diagnosis and Treatment
of Five Common Ailments*

W. Scott Moore

Eleos Press

Rogersville, Alabama

First Edition

R for the Rural Church

Author: W. Scott Moore, B.B.A, M. Div., D. Min.
© 2014 by Eleos Press www.eleospress.com

Cover Art: W. Scott Moore
Cover Design: W. Scott Moore
Interior Formatting: Eleos Press www.eleospress.com

Also available in eBook form

Eleos Press publishes this volume as a document of critical, theological, historical, and/or literary significance and does not necessarily endorse or promote all the views or statements made herein, or verify the accuracy of any statements made by the Author. References to persons or incidents herein may have been changed to protect the identity of those involved.

ISBN-13: 978-0692301685

PRINTED IN THE UNITED STATES OF AMERICA

NOTE TO THE READER

I served as the Associate Pastor of the Pleasant Grove Baptist Church in Moulton, Alabama, from 1984 – 1987 and from 1992 – 1999. The pastor, Jackie Shelton, had a vision of building "the Greatest Rural Church in America." Under his leadership, the church membership quadrupled from 488 members in 1980 to 1,980 members in 2004. During that same time period, total receipts increased by an astronomical 1400 percent, from $65,546.00 to $925,766.00. Sunday school average attendance for the church more than tripled from 153 to 516.

The five sections of this book were written during my final four years at Pleasant

Grove Baptist Church—1996 – 1999. They are the product of five of six doctoral seminars. By the grace of God, and with the prompting of my lovely wife, Diane, I received my doctorate from the Mid-America Baptist Theological Seminary in Cordova, Tennessee, in 2003.

TABLE OF CONTENTS

FOREWORD

A pastor friend confided, "The day in and day out demands of the pastorate wear on me. What can I do to keep myself fresh?" His dilemma resonated with me. What pastor doesn't relate to that issue?

My friend and I discussed some ways to keep ourselves "at the ready" for the pastoral task. Fellowship with other pastors, training conferences, the practice of spiritual disciplines, family time all entered the conversation. We also agreed that reading what other pastors write about ministry can be invigorating.

Pastor, you will find this book by W. Scott Moore to be one of those volumes that enhances your ministry. It will inform you about certain aspects of the pastor's role such as prayer and preaching. It will challenge you to think about possible ways to build teams and facilitate church growth. It will offer practical guidance for specific church situations like church discipline.

The scholarly approach to the development of this book is of value. A Biblical foundation is laid for most of the guidance offered. This will make you "dig deep" in a way that will be good for you.

That which commends this work above all else is that it comes from a pastor's heart. I have known Scott Moore for almost thirty years. We served together in neighboring churches for many of those years. I grew to appreciate Scott's dedication to the Lord, his commitment to the pastoral calling, and his friendship.

As you digest this book, you will get a sense that the writer has "been there." He lives and ministers by the suggestions in this handbook. Scott loves other pastors. He does not claim to provide every answer to every situation pastors face. But you will find helpful information that will refresh your heart as you go about the high calling of pastor.

Darryl Wood, Th.D.
Pastor, First Baptist Church
Vincent, Alabama

INTRODUCTION

My wife and I grew up in the sprawling metropolis of Atlanta, Georgia. We both attended, and graduated from, the University of Georgia in Athens, Georgia. We moved to Memphis, Tennessee, so that I could attend the Mid-America Baptist Theological Seminary.

Imagine our surprise when, upon my graduation, our first church would be a church in *Moulton*, Alabama. Rather, the church was located in *Wren*, Alabama, a tiny community located three miles south of Moulton.

Since those early days, I have enjoyed the privilege—and it *has been* a privilege—of serving in rural churches for 25 of my 30 years in Christian ministry. I have particularly grown to enjoy the unhurried atmosphere in the rural church.

Luke notes the response of the rulers, elders, and scribes in Acts 4:13:

> *Now as they observed the confidence of Peter and John and understood that they were uneducated and untrained men, they were amazed, and began to recognize them as having been with Jesus.*

In the same way I believe that you, my reader, like Peter and John, are intelligent, knowledgeable, and prayerful men and women of God. It is with that understanding that I present to you this oftentimes detailed, and somewhat scholarly, volume. I believe that you, my dear brothers and sisters, can handle it!

A companion volume to <u>Rural Revival: Growing Churches in Shrinking Communities</u>, this book is designed to help you, the rural pastor, leader, or church member to improve your prayer life, preaching (for the pastors), grow your church, and deal with the day-to-day opportunities and problems that you will ultimately face.

May God bless you as we labor together to lead and to grow His churches.

AILMENT ONE: PRAYERLESSNESS

Rural church leadership is an extremely demanding task. Bible study and prayer may seem optional for the other members of a church, but are requirements for church leaders. In particular, the pastor cannot properly meet the challenges of the office without a constant commitment to both personal Bible study and prayer.

The latter discipline, prayer, is the subject of this study. In maintaining an adequate prayer life, church leaders should have an understanding of the following: the definition of prayer, the two-way communication involved in prayer, the types of prayer appropriate to the various developmental stages of the Christian life, the need for continuously setting new goals in prayer when previous goals have been reached, and a prayer outline to organize their prayer lives.

Definition of Prayer

Prayer is a term that is much used and often misunderstood. Many see it as only an attempt to persuade God to act according to the desires of the petitioner.

Some Christians believe prayer is something observed occasionally, such as before meals or going to bed. A popular definition misrepresents prayer as "an address (as a petition) to God . . . in word or thought."[1]

The best understanding of the meaning of prayer can be found in the Bible. Definitions of the five Old Testament and the three New Testament words most commonly translated as "prayer" (in the King James Version of the Bible) are helpful.

Old Testament Words for Prayer

Five Old Testament words for prayer are: ראהתא, and האיש, השאהאל, לאלאפ, האללהפת.

---

[1] Merriam Webster's Collegiate Dictionary, 10th Edition (Springfield, MA: Merriam-Webster, Inc., 1995), 914.

האלל◻ה is the most widely used Old Testament word for prayer, employed in that capacity a total of seventy-seven times. האללהפ means "[to] pray a prayer[,] a house of prayer[, or to] hear [a] prayer."[2]

The four words האיש, השאהאל, לאלאפ, and ראהתא are translated prayer only once each. לאלאﬧ, rendered prayer seventy-four times, means "to intercede [or] to pray."[3] השאהאל, means "[the] whisper[ing] (of [a] prayer)."[4] האי◻ש has the idea of "meditation,

---

[2] R. Laird Harris, Gleason L. Archer, Jr., and Bruce K. Waltke, eds. <u>Theological Wordbook of the Old Testament</u>, vol. A (Chicago: Moody Press, 1980), 1776.

[3] Ibid., 1776.

[4] Ibid., 1107.

complaint, [or] musing[; to] talk."[5]   ראההתא,
means "to pray, entreat, supplicate[;] to make
supplication, [to] plead."[6]

The Old Testament idea of prayer, then,
is much broader than the popular definition of
petition. It also includes the place of prayer, the
listening aspect of prayer, prayer for the needs
of others, and meditation.

──────────────

[5] Harris, Theological Wordbook of the Old Testament.,
2255.

[6] Ibid., 1722.

W. Scott Moore

NEW TESTAMENT WORDS FOR PRAYER

There are three New Testament words and their derivatives translated as prayer in the King James Version of the Bible. They are: προσευκη, δεησισ, and εντευξισ. The most commonly used word (thirty-nine times), προσευκη, means a "prayer addressed to God."[7]

The second word most widely translated as prayer is the word δεησισ. Used twelve times, δεησισ means "seeking, asking, entreating, entreaty."[8]

---

[7] Joseph Henry Moore, <u>Greek-English Lexicon of the New Testament</u> (Grand Rapids: Zondervan Publishing House, 1981), 545.

[8] Greek-English Lexicon of the New Testament, 126.

A third word, εντευξισ, means prayer only twice in the New Testament. Εντευξισ carries the idea of "an interview, a coming together . . ., that for which an interview is held, a conference or conversation, a petition, supplication."[9] This word is helpful in recognizing the two-way aspect of communication with God.

Besides their general definitions, Thayer[10] compares the three synonyms. He gives them the following shades of meaning: προσευκη "is unrestricted in its contents," is "limited to prayer to God," and includes "the element of devotion."

---

[9] Ibid., 132.

[10] Ibid., 126.

Δεησισ, on the other hand, is primarily petitionary. It may "be used of a request addressed to man," and "gives prominence to the expression of personal need." Εντευξισ "expresses confiding access to God." It centers on the "childlike confidence" a believer should have when entering the presence of God.

The New Testament usage, therefore, adds two thoughts to both the Old Testament idea and the popular definition. One thought involves the idea of pleading with God. This extends the concept of prayer to more than just a dispassionate statement of one's need to God.

The other thought found exclusively in the New Testament is that of a "conference with God." The petitioner speaks with God, confident that God is truly listening.

Two-Way Communication

Most church leaders understand the art of speaking to God in prayer. Many, however, need to learn to listen to God through a systematic study of the Bible. God's Holy Spirit will answer many prayers by bringing to one's remembrance the specific word (ρημα) needed for the specific situation. Jesus says in Matthew 4:4, "It is written, 'man shall not live by bread alone, but by every word that proceedeth out of the mouth of God.'" The term ρημα, translated word, means "a constituent part of speech or writing . . . [that can be] distinguished from the contents as a whole."[11]

Prayer, for two reasons, must not be a unidirectional activity. First, pastors need to listen to God as followers of Jesus. Spiritual maintenance and growth are dependent upon the leadership of the Holy Spirit in prayer.

Second, church leaders should listen to God to receive instruction after moving onto the church field. They constantly need to request the Lord's leadership regarding the messages they preach. This practice is helpful in majoring on more than one or two topics ("hobby horses"). It is also helpful in

---

[11] Marvin R. Vincent, <u>Word Studies in the New Testament</u> (Grand Rapids: Wm. B. Eerdmans Publishing Co., 1989), vol. 1, 260.

maintaining integrity while under personal attacks from church members when retaliating from the pulpit can become attractive.

They also need to continue to seek God's guidance on the church field in the ways they relate to the members of their church. It is easy for pastors to minister to those who show their appreciation, but much more difficult to minister to those who oppose their ministry and leadership. Prayer enables pastors to display the love of God to members who are antagonistic toward their ministries.

Prayer on the church field also equips church leaders in their positiona of leadership in the church. Those who regularly seek the Lord in prayer will consistently make wise decisions, and find that the church members are more likely to follow them. Church leaders can then move beyond simply following their instincts. They will also find assistance in achieving God's calling with His authority.

THE STAGES OF THE CHRISTIAN LIFE

Beginnings

The Christian life must begin with prayer. Salvation is always associated with some form of prayer. According to Romans 10:13, "for whosoever shall call upon the name of the Lord shall be saved." The word in the original language is επικαλεομαι, which means:

> *to call upon by pronouncing the name of Jehovah. [This] expression find[s] its*

explanation in the fact that prayers addressed to God ordinarily began with an invocation of the divine name.[12]

The same word, επικαλεομαι, is used in Acts 2:21. A group of prospective converts was admonished: "whosoever shall call on the name of the Lord shall be saved."

The Apostle Paul encountered the Lord on the road to Damascus. His conversion occurred while talking with the Lord. Paul said, "Lord, what wilt thou have me to do?" (Acts 9:6)

Cornelius, the first Gentile convert (Acts 10), prayed before his salvation. Προσευχη is the word used to describe his prayer (see above). The Lord sent Simon Peter to share the gospel

---

[12] Vincent, <u>Word Studies in the New Testament</u>, vol. 3, 496.

with him and, in response to the prayer, he and his family were saved (Acts 10:31).

Paul challenged Lydia, the first Philippian believer, to trust in Christ for salvation at a place where people (προσευκη) customarily offered up prayers to the Lord (Acts 16:13). Because of her prayer, her "heart [was] opened [by the Lord]," and she listened to Paul; she and her family responded and placed their faith in Jesus Christ.

Initial Growth

Christians establish a basic relationship with God as they seek to know God personally through prayer. New converts, therefore, have a tremendous need to speak with God.

Young Christians should also spend time in prayer because God particularly delights in hearing from them. Great faith is a mark of their prayers (Luke 18:16; Matt. 18:3). God is pleased with their faith (Heb. 11:6).

A baby Christian in Athens, Georgia, heard Bertha Smith speak about the Shantung Revival in China. He had a great desire to learn more about God through an association with her, and so asked the Lord to let them spend time together.

Older, and more mature, Christians spoke to the young man. They attempted to explain the reasons why his prayer request was impractical. His faith, however, was undaunted and God honored his prayer. Miss Bertha selected him during the summer of 1982 to be

her personal valet for her speaking engage-
ments.

New Christians need to develop a prayer
life because of the danger of becoming legalistic
in their Christian lives. Two of the
characteristics of a Spirit-led life are freedom
and joy in Christ. Once prayer is no longer
being practiced, a Christian can easily begin a
life of rules and regulations (Gal. 3). The same
grace offered at salvation is available throughout
the Christian life to those who build a
relationship with the Lord through prayer.

Maturity

Maturity in prayer is, first, characterized
by obedience. Jesus, in prayer, stated His
voluntary obedience to the Father in the

Garden of Gethsemane (Mark 14:36). Jesus throughout His earthly ministry, though equal to the Heavenly Father, willingly submitted to His Father's direction (Phil. 2:5-8).

An attribute of the prayer of mature Christians is a focus on the needs of other Christians. Jesus set the example when He made several requests for His followers (John 17). His famous high priestly prayer included a prayer for the essential ingredient of unity (vs. 11). He wanted for His church to have a singleness of purpose to both reach the world of unsaved people and provide the nurturing environment essential for proper spiritual growth.

The Lord also prayed that believers would remain in the world system. Mature believers also need to pray for new Christians to interact with lost people. This needs to be done without allowing the world system to find or reestablish a place in their unseasoned spiritual lives (vv. 15-16).

Experienced Christians, like Jesus, know that other Christians need protection from ο πονηροσ, the evil one. They need to pray for young Christians. Satan wants to bring "toils, annoyances, and perils . . . to [the] Christian['s] faith and steadfastness [and his desire to cause] pain and trouble."[13]

Jesus further prayed for the sanctification of all Christians. He wanted to sanctify them, or set them apart, by the truth. Christians should

---

[13] Gerhard Friedrich, ed., Theological Dictionary of the New Testament, vol. 6 (Grand Rapids: Wm. B. Eerdmans Publishing Co., 1974), 546.

pray for each other to begin and maintain the search for truth in the written Word that is truth—the Bible.   The Bible is essential for spiritual growth, as demonstrated in I Pet. 2:2: "As newborn babes, desire the sincere milk of the word, that ye may grow thereby."

Calling and Commissioning to Ministry

The skill of listening to God is essential in the pastor's call to the ministry. The calling to the ministry must be from God. It should never become either one's personal desire to enter the ministry or the recommendation of other people of a suitable career choice.

A functional prayer life is essential for one whom God calls into the preaching ministry to clearly hear and follow the calling. Pastors are personally chosen, or called out, by God for the particular task He has selected for them to do. Paul prayed for God's direction (Acts 9:6); Jesus responded by articulating His calling for Paul in Acts 9:15b: "he is a chosen vessel unto me, to bear my name before the Gentiles, and kings, and the children of Israel."

The local church is the Lord's commissioning agent (Acts 13:2) and must also be aware of God's calling upon a pastor's life. A local church validates the calling and must, therefore, have an adequate corporate prayer life.

Years of Ministry

A great tragedy in Christendom today is the loss of ministerial effectiveness by mature, godly pastors. This not only affects pastors but also those who follow and respect them.

The Apostle Paul states his concern regarding being disqualified from the ministry. He says in I Cor. 9:27: "But I keep under my body, and bring it into subjection: lest that by any means, when I have preached to others, I myself should be castaway."

The greatest potential for disqualification is in the area of the flesh. Pastors who commit the sins of the flesh listed in Gal. 5:19-21 will eventually find that they are incapable of effectively serving God in the ministry.

Ministers who have specific problems with sexual sins cannot continue to legitimately function in their pastoral roles. A life of immorality "is fairly easy to maintain because there are no obvious signs of the addiction as there is with drug or alcohol abuse."[14] An impure life is a tremendous betrayal of pastors' trust from God, their spouses, and the members of their congregations.

Pastors cannot serve other gods if they wish to remain in their ministries. Pastors who make decisions based on financial considerations, prominence of position, or personal career objectives will forfeit the

---

[14] Steve Gallagher, Tearing Down the High Places of Sexual Idolatry (Crittendon, KY: Pure Life Press, 1986), 15

confidence needed to maintain influence with their parishioners.

A chemical dependency also weakens the credibility of pastors. Paul wrote in I Cor. 6:12b, "All things are lawful for me, but I will not be brought under the power of any." Christian leaders who succumb to addictive substances cannot follow the admonition to follow the leadership of the Holy Spirit (Eph. 5:18). They are not, consequently, equipped to lead others.

Seasoned pastors, subsequently, should never become comfortable with a life of prayerlessness. Too much is at stake to potentially sacrifice a life's work through the spiritual lethargy and capacity for sin which result from a neglect of prayer. They must maintain a viable prayer life not only throughout their years of ministry, but also until the Lord calls them home to Heaven.

GOAL-SETTING IN PRAYER

Appropriate goals are necessary for every part of the Christian endeavor. Pastors must establish objectives to grow in any area of their lives. According to Zig Ziglar, former vice-president of the Southern Baptist Convention and a motivational speaker, there are "several different kinds of goals: physical, financial, spiritual, career, family, mental, and social."[15]

There are three perspectives that are helpful in recognizing the need for establishing

---

[15] Zig Ziglar, <u>See You at the Top</u>, 155.

goals in one's prayer life. The first perspective is a definition of the word in its general usage. A second perspective is an examination of the scriptural accounts of several characters in the Bible. Their lives clearly show the need for goals.

Simply knowing the definition and application to the lives of Bible characters is insufficient. The third perspective, therefore, deals with the need for pastors to set personal goals in their lives today.

Definition of a Goal

A goal is "the end toward which effort is directed; the aim."[16]   Two New Testament Greek forms of the same word relate well to the idea of a goal. One form, a verb, is the word σκοπεω. Σκοπεω occurs only six times in the New Testament. The word contextually means "to pay attention to" in all six verses. Thayer defines σκοπεω as "to look at, observe, or contemplate, to mark."[17]

Another form, a noun, is the word σκοποσ. This word may be translated "an

---

[16] Merriam-Webster's Collegiate Dictionary, 10th edition, 499.

[17] Greek-English Lexicon of the New Testament, 579.

observer, a watchman, the distant mark looked at, the goal or end one has in view."[18]

For pastors, then a goal is the focus of their attention. Prayer is crucial in evaluating the appropriateness of goals and in determining the proper process in reaching those goals.

Bible Characters

Several personalities in the Bible show the need for goals in maintaining a prayer life. These characters include the Old Testament figure of Elijah and the New Testament figures of John the Baptist and the Apostle Paul.

---

[18] Ibid., 579.

W. Scott Moore

ELIJAH

Elijah prayed for the rain and dew to be withheld for a period. He continued praying throughout the resulting period of drought to detect the Lord's leadership in restoring the rainfall. Three-and-one-half years passed before he received a subsequent word from the Lord, when God showed His power through Elijah in eradicating Baal worship in Israel.

Elijah felt he had completed his task since he had accomplished his major goals. A threat from Jezebel sent him to Beer-sheba in the southern tribe of Judah. There he showed several signs of one who has accomplished a major task and needed to find new goals: a willingness to die (I Kings 19:4), a need for a great deal of sleep (vs. 5, 6), and a feeling of being alone in his mission (vv. 10, 14).

The Lord, being omniscient, understood Elijah's plight. He immediately established three new goals. First, Elijah was to anoint Hazael king over Syria. Second, he was to anoint Jehu king over Israel. Third, he was to anoint Elisha as his successor in the prophetic ministry.

JOHN THE BAPTIST

John the Baptist was a second Bible personality who accomplished his prayer goals and needed further direction. He had spent many years in the desert in preparation for his public ministry—characterized by a message of repentance.

He fulfilled his mission of preparation for the coming of Jesus. John had invested enough time in prayer with the Lord that he knew the sign of Jesus' coming (John 1:33). He acknowledged that Jesus was "the Son of God (John 1:34)."

John knew that his primary calling of preparation for the Messiah was complete. He was then willing to relinquish the spotlight and serve in a lesser position (John 3:30).

He continued preaching his message of repentance and was arrested by Herod for challenging the king's adulterous affair. His ministry goals apparently accomplished, he questioned Jesus' Messianic position (Matt. 11:2-3). He desperately wanted to establish the fact that his ministry had been profitable. Jesus sent word back through John's disciples that He was fulfilling all of the signs attributed through the Old Testament prophecies to the Anointed One of Israel. John's ministry was then completed; he had successfully paved the way for Jesus and His ministry.

THE APOSTLE PAUL

The Apostle Paul was never satisfied with achievements (Phil. 3:13-14). He was always striving to reach more people for the Lord. Once, he wanted to go to Asia to spread the gospel (Acts 16). He, through prayer, was told that God did not want his group to go there. He then went to Mysia, and desired to go to Bithynia. Again the Lord, through prayer, told him not to go.

God responded to Paul's prayer, and led the group to Macedonia. The church at Philippi was established as the company of Christians, under Paul's leadership, followed God's direction through prayer.

The Need for Goals

Pastors have a tremendous need to set personal goals in their prayer lives. Someone has said that "the person who aims at nothing will hit it every time." Those who have no goals in prayer will never move beyond their current circumstances to find any real measure of spiritual success. They will live chaotic lives, hoping everything will somehow improve.

Goals are necessary, therefore, in the establishment of direction for spiritual growth and ministry, in monitoring progress, in the development of a sense of personal and corporate achievement, and in sustaining the motivation to pray. Spiritual growth and ministry must be determined after seeking the Lord's guidance in prayer. According to R. A. Torrey, an American evangelist and Bible scholar, "we can often bring more to pass by praying than we can by any other form of effort we might put forth."[19]

Pastors should never limit themselves to personal experience. Past successes and failures are poor indicators of the present and future. Past successes, or victories, have the capacity to

---

[19] R. A. Torrey, The Power of Prayer (Grand Rapids, Zondervan Publishing Co., 1971), 27.

become hindrances to God's plan for pastors in their future ministries (Phil. 3:13-14). Outstanding former achievements have the capacity to lull pastors into a sense of complacency. They begin to believe they have already accomplished enough for God and no longer need to seek His leadership for the future.

Past failures, on the other hand, have the same delimiting effect. Pastors who continually undergo monumental defeats in their ministries without maintaining their prayer lives will often capitulate. God uses the difficulties of today to test a pastor's faith and then later transforms them into provisions for success. Prayer is indispensable in detecting the point at which this transformation occurs. Prayer also places the defeats in perspective and provides the impetus for seeking and securing future victories.

God is also a God of order (I Cor. 14:33). He has a definite plan for each pastor's personal growth. He wants to express that plan to His leaders. According to David Seamands, Professor of Pastoral Ministries at Asbury Theological Seminary, "Our dreams, aspirations, and visions are often God-given and are one of His ways of communicating with us."[20] Some pastors may need to seek the Lord's direction for improvement in personal Bible study; others may be deficient in the area of soul-winning. God assesses the individual need

---

[20] David A. Seamands, Living with Your Dreams (Wheaton, IL: Victor Books, 1990) ,16

and, through prayer, directs the pastor in carrying out the steps toward fulfillment of that need.

Prayer is irreplaceable in monitoring progress toward God-given goals. Pastors are, often, too absorbed by their work to observe it from the proper perspective. Prayer enables pastors to obtain God's point of view. According to Peter Lord, retired pastor of the Park Avenue Baptist Church in Titusville, Florida: "Our heavenly Father knows the *truth* about the 'object of our attention.' He has complete insight into the matter."[21]

---

[21] Peter Lord, Hearing God (Grand Rapids: Baker Book House Co., 1988), 178.

Pastors also need to set personal and corporate goals in prayer to develop a sense of achievement. Ministry is often a thankless occupation. Pastors rarely receive the praise they deserve for the labors they perform in their churches. They can become discouraged unless they turn to the Lord in prayer.

God-given goals effectively change the hopelessness of many personal ministry situations into the minor setbacks that they really are. God is, by His very nature, an Encourager. This is apparent because the Holy Spirit is the Giver of all of the spiritual gifts, including the gift of exhortation or encouragement (Rom. 12:8). Prayer allows pastors to receive the encouragement they need from God. They are thereby equipped to continue to minister in often unfriendly environments.

Prayer goals not only help pastors to be personally encouraged about their own particular ministries, but also to understand the ways in which their contributions work on a corporate level. God helps pastors to have the total view of His work needed to motivate them to remain faithful in His service. He uses this overall view to furnish pastors with the goals needed for their continued participation in building His kingdom.

Pastors require goals to maintain the motivation needed to sustain their prayer lives. Purposeful prayer with tangible, quantifiable results is much more rewarding than a disorganized prayer life. Clear objectives in prayer allow pastors to recognize answers to prayer and, consequently, to keep their commitment to a life of prayer.

W. Scott Moore

SUGGESTED PRAYER OUTLINE

Prayer, like any other Christian discipline, needs to be organized to be effective. The following concepts, taken from the book of the Revelation, are possible means for pastors to structure their prayer lives.

There are four "in the Spirit" passages in the book: Revelation 1:10, Revelation 4:2, Revelation 17:3, and Revelation 21:10. These four passages, or divisions, may be identified as four of the five parts of a pastor's prayer time.

The first part, confession, is based upon Revelation 1:10: "What thou seest, write in a book, and send it unto the seven churches." The churches each had a particular sin (or implied sin) for which they were being corrected. Pastors begin each prayer session with confession of personal and corporate sin.

The second part, praise, is found in Revelation 4:2. This passage states: ". . . and, behold, a throne was set in heaven, and one sat on the throne." The throne room of Heaven, with God Himself on the throne, elicits the praise of anyone who is invited there. Pastors now enter a state of praise for the One who is worthy of all praise.

The third division is that of the actual request, or petition, of the believer. Revelation 17:3a states: "So he carried me away in the spirit into the wilderness." This wilderness is a place where several spiritual needs are presented. Pastors may now begin a time of sharing their needs with their Heavenly Father.

The fourth division is the place of the blessing. "And he carried me away in the spirit to a great and high mountain, and showed me that great city, the holy Jerusalem, descending out of heaven from God (Revelation 21:10)." The greatest blessing believers will ever know is that of being united with their Bride-groom, Jesus Christ, forever in the New Jerusalem that the Heavenly Father has created for them. Pastors, therefore, use this division of their prayer time for receiving the blessings that the Lord wants to give them.

The final division is worship. Worship is simply silence and reverence before God. This category of prayer time is the time when pastors can find rest in the presence of the Lord.

There are seven days in a week; a prayer life, to be both balanced and challenging, could have a different theme each day. The seven letters to the churches, found in the Book of the Revelation, provide a good basis for the different themes for the seven days in a given week.

The theme for Sunday, the first day of the week, is a good example. The first of the seven letters is written to the church at Ephesus (Revelation 2:1-7). The confession section comes from the statement that the church had "left its first love." Pastors should confess, therefore, that they may have personally or corporately (as a church or nation) moved away from the initial love they once had for their Savior. They need to examine themselves to see if they have developed Christian habits—doing the Christian duties, without the resultant joy.

The praise for Sunday comes from the description of Jesus as the one who "holds the seven stars" in His right hand, who is "in the midst of the seven golden candle-sticks." He now receives praise as the One Who dwells in the *midst* of His people, and protects each of His churches.

The request is taken from the admonition that Christians should "remember, repent, and do the works" they did when they first trusted Jesus Christ as Lord and Savior. They ask Him, therefore, to help them to be obedient in following Him.

The blessing described in the passage is that Christians will be invited to "eat of the tree of life." God wants believers to not only receive eternal life, but also that they will presently experience the abundant life (John 10:10).

CONCLUSION

A sustained prayer life is one of the most crucial prerequisites for ministry. Many pastors are losing their privileges to minister through the commission of various sins. A primary factor causing such disqualification is prayerlessness.

Other pastors are struggling with a lack of vision for their ministries. Prayer is essential in finding, shaping, and maintaining a vision from God.

Still others are just waiting for retirement, convinced that ministry is simply another profession. They do not believe that God wants to equip and energize them for ministry.

Prayer is, therefore, essential to properly function in the pastoral role. Pastors must first find leadership from God, and then can begin to adequately lead their churches.

AILMENT TWO: LACK OF BIBLICAL PREACHING

Many groups move into heresy by decontextualizing certain verses of the Bible. The Church of Christ is an example of this type of doctrinal error. Their basic tenet, baptismal regeneration, is based upon such verses as Mark 16:16, Acts 2:38, and Acts 22:16.

The third verse, Acts 22:16, declares: "And now why tarriest thou? Arise, and be baptized, and wash away thy sins, calling on the name of the Lord." This verse is the final verse in a paragraph beginning with Acts 22:12.[22]

This study is based upon Acts 22:12-16. It will use the components of the exegetical pyramid. The exegetical pyramid is a useful tool in the study of a Biblical passage. The study will conclude with the actual sermon outline with accompanying illustrations.

EXEGETICAL PYRAMID

The Exegetical Pyramid is composed of several parts. They are: the contextual analysis, the variants analysis, the syntactical analysis, the

---

[22] United Bible Societies, <u>The Greek New Testament</u>, 3d ed. (New York: American Bible Society, 1975), 506-507.

verbal analysis, the literary analysis, the theological analysis, the homiletical analysis, and the final synthesis.[23]

Contextual Analysis

The first section of the exegetical pyramid is the contextual analysis. This includes the background information of the passage and the pertinent details found in the surrounding verses and chapters. The author of both the books of Luke and Acts was Luke. The key characters involved in this passage of

---

[23] Dale Ellenburg, "Doctor of Ministry Seminar: Interpretation/Preaching," notebook of materials from a seminar sponsored by Mid-America Baptist Theological Seminary (Memphis, TN) 28 October, 1997, photocopied.

Acts were the Apostle Paul and Ananias. Paul's audience was a gathering of Jews in Asia and a group of Roman soldiers who had arrested Paul for apparently inciting a riot in the temple (Acts 21:27, 31).

This incident occurred at the conclusion of Paul's third missionary journey.[24] He had departed from Miletus, where he had given the people a final farewell. He went through Cos, Rhodes, Patara, Phoenicia, Cyprus, Syria, Tyre, Ptolemais, and Caesarea. Paul received several warnings of the danger that awaited him in Jerusalem. He spent the night in Jerusalem,

---

[24] Stanley D. Toussaint, "Acts," in Bible Knowledge Commentary, New Testament edition, eds. John V. Walvoord and Roy B. Zuck (Wheaton, IL: Victor Books, 1983), 415.

discussed the requirements for Gentile believers with the elders of the church, and went to the temple.

The Jews saw Paul in the temple, and attempted to kill him. A group of Roman soldiers intervened, and arrested Paul.

Paul used his Roman citizenship as leverage for allowing him to make a defense of his position. He was given the opportunity to defend his actions.

Paul's defense, however, was simply an opportunity to share the gospel. He began to build a "bridge" using points of similarity with his Jewish audience. First, he gained their attention by speaking in their native Hebrew language.

Second, he established several points of identification with the crowd. He discussed his background in Judaism including his studies under Gamaliel, a respected leader in the Jewish community (Acts 22:3).

Paul, like his audience, had been a zealous defender of Judaism (Acts 22:4). He, as a matter of public record, had been a chief persecutor of Christianity (Acts 22:4-5). He had already taken several Christians to prison and, at the point of his encounter with Christ, was taking others to a similar fate.

His reference to Ananias said that Ananias "was a devout man according to the law, having a good report of all the Jews which dwelt there." (Acts 22:12) Ananias, therefore, would have been readily accepted by this group of Jews.

Third, he appealed to them on a "what would you have done" basis. He was blinded by a bright light, followed by a voice saying: "Saul, Saul, why persecutest thou me?" Saul asked about the identity of the one who was addressing him, to which Jesus replied: "I am Jesus the Nazarene whom you are persecuting." Paul exercised the only logical option at this point—he asked what Jesus wanted from him and then obeyed.

Variants Analysis

The second component of the exegetical pyramid is an analysis of the variant readings in the passage. There are two questionable readings found in the Acts 22:12-16 passage. The first is found in verse 12: katoikountwn Ioudaiwn. This is the accepted reading found in the King James Version of the Bible, which states: "Jews which dwelt there." Both the New American Standard and New International versions concur with "who lived there" and "living there" respectively.

The United Bible Societies give this a "C" reading. They state that: "The letter 'C' means that there is a considerable degree of doubt whether the text or the apparatus contains the superior reading."[25] The Greek manuscript evidence that supports this reading includes p74, a collection that contains both the book of Acts and the Catholic Epistles. It is dated in the 7th century and, as such, may have a high degree of textual variance.[26]

---

[25] United Bible Societies, The Greek New Testament, xiii.

[26] Ibid., xv.

The scholars have observed that the following Greek uncials also support this reading: a—dated in the 4th century, A—a 5th century document, B—from the 4th century document, E—the 6th century, and P—the 6th century.[27]

The following Greek minuscules also support the reading: 88 (a 12th century document), and 1877 (a 14th century document).[28]

Other supporting evidence includes a part of the Byzantine manuscript tradition. It also includes two sources from Itala, or Old

---

[27] United Bible Societies, <u>The Greek New Testament</u>, xv-xvi.

[28] Ibid., xix-xx.

Latin, which are: e, a 6th century document, and gig, a 13th century document.[29]

Another source that supports this reading, from the 4th and 5th centuries, is the Vulgate (when the Clementine and Wordsworth-White editions are in agreement). The Syriac Peshitta (4th to 7th centuries), the Coptic Bohairic (3rd and 4th centuries), the Armenian (5th century), and the Georgian (5th century) also favor this reading.[30]

An alternate reading is simply Ιουδαιων. This means "all the Jews," and leaves off the word κατοικουντων, meaning: "which dwelt

---

[29] Ibid., xxvii-xxxiii.

[30] United Bible Societies, The Greek New Testament, xxxiv-xxxv.

there." Support for this variant reading includes the following sources: one Greek minuscule—629 (dated in the 14th century), d—an Itala, or Old Latin manuscript (dated in the 5th century), and is found in Chrysostom's writings in the year 407.[31]

Other variant readings include κατοικουντων εν Δαμασκω Ιουδαιων, meaning "all the Jews which dwelt in Damascus." The best evidence for this reading is p41, an 8th century document, which adds the phrase εν τη. This appends the words "in the" and therefore means: "all the Jews which dwelt in the Damascus." q, a Greek uncial dated between

---

[31] United Bible Societies, <u>The Greek New Testament</u>, xix-xxxvii.

the 8th and 9th centuries, also supports this reading.[32]

The variants for verse 12 are not significant in the explanation of the passage. The phrase "who dwelt there" obviously refers to "Damascus" in verse 11. So, whether "Damascus" is clearly stated or simply referenced is relatively insignificant.

The second occurrence of a textual variant within this passage is found in verse 13. The given reading, εισ αυτον, has also been assigned a "C" element of certainty. The strongest support for this reading is p74, a 7th century manuscript.[33] The translators of the

---

[32] Ibid., xiv-xvii.

[33] United Bible Societies, <u>The Greek New Testament</u>, xv.

King James version translated the verse using this reading by stating: "upon him." The New American Standard version also uses this reading with "at him."

One variant reading omits the word ειϭ ("upon"). This makes little sense, as it would be translated *"I looked up* [emphasis added] him." The New International version apparently accepts this reading, and smooths it out with "*I was able to see* [emphasis added] him." This is not materially different from the idea found in the preferred reading. It appears as simply a desire to be different for difference's sake from the other translations of the Bible.

The other variant reading leaves out the whole phrase altogether. This meaning would be significantly different from the preferred reading. The direction of the "looking up," or

αναβλεψον, would be undefined. The strongest support for this variant is contained in an
8th century manuscript, p41.[34]

There is a little support for the variants,
and a difficulty in the resultant translation of
verses 12 and 13. The evidence, therefore,
would warrant favor for the chosen readings.

Syntactical Analysis

The third section of the exegetical
pyramid is the syntactical analysis. Professor
Harold T. Bryson, professor of Preaching and
Director of the Institute of Christian Ministry at
Mississippi College, states: "syntax studies how

---

[34] United Bible Societies, <u>The Greek New Testament</u>, xiv.

words, phrases, and clauses relate to each other."[35] This includes such things as a study of the word order and an identification of the parts of speech.[36]

CONNECTIVES

A connective is a clue to the various divisions of thought within the passage. This passage contains several connective words. The first, "and," is found in all five verses. It is used as a continuative—a word that maintains the flow of the discourse in the previous verses.

---

[35] Harold T. Bryson, Expository Preaching (Nashville: Broadman and Holman Publishers, 1995), 166.

[36] Harold T. Bryson, Expository Preaching, 166.

A second connective is "by," and is found in verse 12. The "standard of the Law" was the means by which Ananias displayed his devotion to his religious heritage.

A third connective is the word "to." This word is found in verses 13, 14, and 15, and always suggests direction. Ananias came and spoke "to" Saul. God had appointed Saul "to" know His will, "to" see His Son, and "to" hear his voice. He was to be a witness "to" all men.

"At" is a fourth connective in this passage. It describes the direction toward which Saul looked—"at" Ananias (verse 13).

A fourth connective is the word "from" in verse 14. The word suggests the direction of the utterance spoken: from Ananias to Saul.

The first word in verse 15, "for," establishes a junction with the statement found in verse 14. God appointed Saul to know, see, and hear "for" the purpose of being his witness.

A final connective, "why" (verse 16), gives the reason for which something is done. Saul was encouraged to immediately ask Jesus for salvation and follow Him in believers' baptism.

ARRANGEMENT OF THE ARGUMENT

A passage may be arranged in either an inductive or deductive manner. According to Dr. Alan Odiam, induction occurs when "particular examples and instances are given first and then summed up by a universal statement."[37]   Deduction, conversely, occurs when:

> *the universal statement is given first and then explained by means of a number of particular examples and instances. When preachers present the thesis first and then follow it with reasons and other explanatory details, they are using a deductive structure.*[38]

The complete passage (Acts 22:1-21) is part of an inductive message. The thesis for the passage is found in verse 21, which stated "Go! For I will send you far away to the Gentiles."

---

[37] Alan Odiam, "Doctor of Ministry Seminar: Interpretation/Preaching," notebook of materials from a seminar sponsored by Mid-America Baptist Theological Seminary (Memphis, TN) 29 October, 1997, photocopied.

[38] Alan Odiam, "Doctor of Ministry Seminar: Interpretation/Preaching," photocopied.

Paul did not reveal the thesis statement until the conclusion of his argument. He wanted to avoid audience hostility until he had fully developed his position.

This specific passage, however, was Paul's account of a message delivered to him by Ananias. Saul had been prepared to listen by the encounter with Jesus. This passage was, therefore, a deductive message with the following thesis: "God appointed Saul to know His will, to see His Son, and to hear His voice so that Saul could testify on His behalf."

VERBAL ANALYSIS

The fourth level of the exegetical pyramid is the verbal analysis. Verbal analysis is the examination of the various words in a given passage.

There are many significant words in this text. They may be divided into several categories: verbs, proper names, nouns, adjectives, and phrases containing several words.

Verbs

An important verb, found in verse 12, is "μαρτυρουμενος." μαρτυρουμενος is the present passive participle of the verb μαρτυρεω. The word μαρτυρεω may be used as a "[legal term], e.g., . . . [one used] in trials or legal transactions."[39] Paul was figuratively placing the Damascene Jews on the witness stand as character witnesses for his key witness, Ananias. The present tense denotes continuous action, or their constant readiness to testify on Ananias' behalf. The testimonies of these "witnesses" would have served to legitimize Paul's conversion experience in the minds of the members of the audience.

Another verb is αναβλεψον, which is a command for Paul "to see again."[40] The

---

[39] H. Strathmann, "Martyreo," in <u>Theological Dictionary of the New Testament</u>, vol. 4, ed. Gerhard Friedrich (Grand Rapids: Wm. B. Eerdmans Publishing Co., 1974), 474.

[40] Giessen Brunnen-Verlag, <u>A Linguistic Key to the Greek New Testament</u>, trans. Fritz Rienecker, ed. Cleon L. Rogers, Jr. (Grand Rapids: Zondervan Publishing House, 1980), 324.

authority to speak such a command, which resulted in Saul's recovery of sight, could only have come from God.

A third verb, found in verse 14, is "προεχειρισατο." προεχειρισατο means: "to take into one's hands beforehand, to plan, to purpose, to determine."[41] This verb was used in the aorist tense. It thus meant that God had personally selected Saul, at a definite point in time before his conversion, for His service.

A fourth verb, γνωναι, is the aorist active infinitive form of the word γινωσκω. γινωσκω

---

[41] Ibid., 324.

means: "to become acquainted with, to know."[42] The word (as opposed to synonyms such as ειδεναι, επιστασθαι, and συνιεναι) "denotes a discriminating apprehension of external impressions, a knowledge grounded in personal experience."[43] Saul would consequently know the will of God on an intimate, personal basis.

Ιδειν is the fifth verb of significance in this passage. ιδειν is the aorist infinitive of the word οραω, and means: "to see . . . physical[ly] .

---

[42] [Carl Ludwig] Grimm and [Christian Gottlob] Wilke, Greek-English Lexicon of the New Testament, trans. and rev. Joseph Henry Thayer (New York: American Book Co., 1889; reprint, Grand Rapids: Zondervan Publishing House, 1981), 117.

[43] Ibid., 118.

. . [with] the discerning mind."[44]   Ananias promised Saul the ability to see and to understand the greatness of Jesus Christ. According to one scholar:

> *Paul actually saw the risen Lord outside Damascus in addition to hearing His voice. . . . The vision of Christ was the central and all-important feature of his conversion-experience.*[45]

Saul was also told he would ακουσαι, or "hear" a word from Jesus. ακουσαι is the aorist infinitive of the verb ακουω. Ananias referred

---

[44] Carl Ludwig] Grimm and [Christian Gottlob] Wilke, Greek-English Lexicon of the New Testament, 451-452.

[45] F. F. Bruce, Commentary on the Book of the Acts, in The New International Commentary on the New Testament. F. F. Bruce, gen. ed. (Grand Rapids: Wm. B. Eerdmans Publishing Co., 1976), 442.

to the fact that Saul, at the point of his encounter with Jesus, had "perceive[d His] voice."[46]

Ananias used the command "βαπτισαι," the aorist middle imperative form of βαπτιζω. βαπτιζω is:

> *used particularly of the rite of sacred ablution, first instituted by John the Baptist, afterwards by Christ's command received by Christians and adjusted to the contents and nature of their religion. . . . [It refers to] an immersion in water, performed as a sign of the removal of sin, and administered to those who, impelled by a desire for salvation, sought admission to the benefits of the Messiah's kingdom.[47]*

---

[46] Carl Ludwig] Grimm and [Christian Gottlob] Wilke, <u>Greek-English Lexicon of the New Testament</u>, 23.

[47] Ibid., 94

Ananias essentially commanded Saul: "Get yourself baptised."[48]

Ananias also commanded Saul to "wash away [his] sins," or απολουσαι. This verb, like βαπτισαι, is used in the aorist middle imperative form. A translation of the word απολουω, in keeping with the contextual meaning, is:

> *to wash off or away. . . . [It is used] figuratively . . . [to describe the one who] obtains remission of sins [and] . . . is cleansed from them in the sight of God.[49]*

---

[48] Giessen Brunnen-Verlag, <u>A Linguistic Key to the Greek New Testament,</u> 324.

[49] Carl Ludwig] Grimm and [Christian Gottlob] Wilke, <u>Greek-English Lexicon of the New Testament</u>, 65.

Proper Names

Many proper names found in the Bible are significant because their meanings often reflect something of the character of the person to whom they refer. One such proper name, contained in verse 12, is "Ἀνανιας." The name is of Hebrew origin, and means: "Jehovah is gracious."[50] The name itself connoted his parents' dedication to the Lord of the Old Testament—a godly heritage. It is noteworthy that he was God's chosen instrument of grace at the point of Saul's conversion.

---

[50] Carl Ludwig] Grimm and [Christian Gottlob] Wilke, Greek-English Lexicon of the New Testament, 40.

"Σαουλ," another proper name of Hebrew origin, means: "asked for."[51] It was "the name of the first king of Israel."[52] King Saul was placed on the throne because the people "asked for" God to give them a king.

Saul, as used in this passage, meant: "the Hebrew name of the Apostle Paul, but occurring only in address."[53] He, by contrast, was chosen by God to carry His Word to the Gentiles.

---

[51] Ibid., 568.

[52] Ibid., 568.

[53] Carl Ludwig] Grimm and [Christian Gottlob] Wilke, <u>Greek-English Lexicon of the New Testament</u>, 568.

Nouns

An important noun is found in verse 14:
ο θεος.

> *The articular usage of* θεος *would have dispelled any doubt as to the identity of the speaker: "the one and only true God.*[54]

The Jewish audience would have known by this reference that Ananias was speaking of their God—the one they worshiped.

A second significant noun, θελημα, is also found in verse 14. θελημα, translated as "will," more precisely means: the result of "be[ing] resolved, . . . be[ing] determined, [or having a]

---

[54] bid., 287.

purpose."[55] Saul would have an experiential knowledge of God's determined will for his life and the lives of others.

Saul was told he would become a μαρτυς for Jesus (verse 15). He would, therefore, be a "witness[:] one who avers, or can aver, what he himself has seen or heard or knows by any other means."[56] Saul was instructed to testify to others concerning his faith in the Lord Jesus Christ.

Adjectives

A significant adjective is "ευλαβην" (verse 12). Ευλαβην refers to the word ανηρ (man). It

---

[55] Carl Ludwig] Grimm and [Christian Gottlob] Wilke, <u>Greek-English Lexicon of the New Testament</u>, 285.

[56] Carl Ludwig] Grimm and [Christian Gottlob] Wilke, <u>Greek-English Lexicon of the New Testament</u>, 392.

is a combination of the words eu—"well or good"[57] and λαμβανω—"to take to one's self, lay hold upon, take possession of."[58] The compound word "is perhaps used mostly for devout Jews because of the element of nervous caution, which is most appropriate where regard must be had for the law."[59] Ananias, therefore, took seriously his Jewish faith and was not a renegade Jew.

Another adjective worthy of note is found in verse 13: αδελφε. αδελφοσ, translated

---

[57] Ibid., 256.

[58] Ibid., 370.

[59] R. Bultman, "Eulabes," in <u>Theological Dictionary of the New Testament</u>, vol. 2, ed. Gerhard Friedrich (Grand Rapids: Wm. B. Eerdmans Publishing Co., 1974), 751.

"brother," "has an OT and Jewish basis."[60] It "reflects the same outlook seen in 22:5 where Jews in Damascus were called the 'brothers' of the Jews in Jerusalem."[61] This is also evident in Acts 3:22, in which the entire nation of Israel is called a "brotherhood" or "family."

A third adjective, found in verse 13, is really a pronoun used adjectivally. The word, "αυτη," refers to the word "ωρα," and means: "the same."[62] The word ωρα means "any

---

[60] H. Von Soden, "Adelphos" in <u>Theological Dictionary of the New Testament,</u> vol. 1, ed. Gerhard Friedrich (Grand Rapids: Wm. B. Eerdmans Publishing Co., 1974), 144.

[61] Stanley D. Toussaint, "Acts," 418.

[62] Carl Ludwig] Grimm and [Christian Gottlob] Wilke, <u>Greek-English Lexicon of the New Testament</u>, 87.

definite time, point of time, moment."[63] The combined word meant that Saul received his sight at the precise moment of Ananias' command. This could not have been coincidental. It was obviously a demonstration of divine healing.

Phrases Containing Several Words

A notable phrase in verse 12 is "κατα τον νομον." This is a limiting expression referring to Ananias' "ευλαβης," or devotion. "τον νομον" is a clear reference to the contents of the Mosaic

---

[63] Ibid., 679.

law.[64] Paul included this word because:

> *it was important to emphasize on the present*
> *occasion that the commission which Paul*
> *received from the risen Christ was to a large*
> *extent communicated by the lips of this pious*
> *and believing Jew, Ananias of Damascus.*[65]

Another phrase, contained in verse 14, is "των πατερων ημων," and may be translated as: "of the fathers of us." "The [title] 'fathers' . . . usually [refers to] the patriarchs. . . . They embody tradition and guarantee covenant grace."[66] Ananias, therefore, reinforced his

---

[64] Carl Ludwig] Grimm and [Christian Gottlob] Wilke, <u>Greek-English Lexicon of the New Testament</u>, 427.

[65] John Phillips, Acts 13-28, vol. 2 in <u>Exploring Acts</u> (Chicago, IL: Moody Press, 1986), 441-442.

[66] G. Schrenk, "Eulabes," in <u>Theological Dictionary of the New Testament</u>, vol. 5, ed. Gerhard Friedrich (Grand Rapids: Wm. B. Eerdmans Publishing Co., 1974), 945.

claim that this was not a different god, but the same God their patriarchal fathers had worshiped.

A third phrase, "επικαλεσαμενος το ονομα αυτου," is also significant. Saul was given the privilege to "call upon," at a definite point in time (aorist tense) for himself (middle voice) "in acknowledging, embracing, [and] professing the name of Christ."[67] This action of "calling" would affect his salvation and wash away his sins.

---

[67] Carl Ludwig] Grimm and [Christian Gottlob] Wilke, <u>Greek-English Lexicon of the New Testament</u>, 448.

Literary Analysis

The fifth component of the exegetical pyramid is the literary analysis of the passage. Sidney Greidanus, professor of preaching and worship at Calvin Theological Seminary in Grand Rapids, Michigan, believes that the book of Acts is just one part of a single volume. This volume, which could be called "Luke-Acts[,] . . . seeks to tell one continuous story."[68] The literary style of Acts is, therefore, comparable to the book of Luke. The two books, once

---

[68] Sidney Greidanus, <u>The Modern Preacher and the Ancient Text</u> (Grand Rapids: Wm. B. Eerdmans Publishing Co., 1988), 283.

considered historical accounts, are now viewed by many as narrative.[69]

The books of Luke and Acts may, however, be more properly classified as historical narratives. They incorporate historical information presented in a narrative form. Gordon D. Fee, professor of New Testament Theology, asserts:

> *Most of the exegetical suggestions given in the preceding chapter ("The Old Testament Narratives") hold true for Acts. What is important here is that Luke was a Gentile, whose inspired narrative is at the same time an excellent example of Hellenistic historiography. . . . Such history was not written simply to keep records or to chronicle the past. Rather it was written both to encourage or entertain . . .*

[69] Ibid., 278.

and to inform, moralize, or offer an apologetic.[70]

The particular passage under study, therefore, is a narrative account of a historical event.

Theological Analysis

The sixth step of the exegetical pyramid is the theological analysis. This step includes an examination of parallel passages in the New Testament. It also includes an examination of

------

[70] Gordon D. Fee and Douglas Stewart, How to Read the Bible for All Its Worth (Grand Rapids: Zondervan Publishing House, 1993), 96.

the doctrine of baptismal regeneration as allegedly supported by Acts 22.

PARALLEL PASSAGES

This passage obviously made reference to the earlier description of Saul's conversion in Acts 9:17-19. Several details found in Acts 22:12-16 were dissimilar from those found in this passage. One reason for this is that most of the description is in the third person, and merely described Saul's compliance with the directives of Acts 22.

A second dissimilarity was the account of the scales falling from Saul's eyes in Acts 9. The extraneous nature of this commentary would not be conducive to the flow of the argument in Acts 22, and was subsequently omitted.

Another parallel passage was the description of Saul's conversion experience in Acts 26:9-23. There was one major difference—there was no mention of Ananias. The reason for this discrepancy is the audience to whom it was delivered. The only people addressed by the Apostle Paul were Herod Agrippa (the king) and Felix (the governor). Neither of these men would have been impressed with the testimony of a devout Israelite named Ananias. His testimony, consequently, was deleted from this passage.

BAPTISMAL REGENERATION

Acts 22:16, as mentioned in the INTRODUCTION, has been used to support the doctrine of baptismal regeneration. This is faulty scholarship for several reasons. First, this passage is in narrative form. Douglas Stewart, a professor of Old Testament at Gordon-Conwell Seminary, stated: a "narrative usually does not directly teach a doctrine."[71] This is significant because baptismal regeneration is a basic tenet of the Church of Christ. The three main verses used to prove this doctrine are all found in either the book of Acts or the Gospels. They are: Mark 16:16, Acts 2:38, and Acts 22:16 and are primarily considered narratives.

Other denominational groups base their beliefs regarding salvation upon supporting passages in the narrative book of Acts. They

---

[71] Gordon D. Fee and Douglas Stewart, How to Read the Bible for All Its Worth, 83.

are, however, diametrically opposed to the
teachings of the Church of Christ. The
Churches of God, the Assemblies of God, et al,
focus on the necessity of the sign gifts for
salvation while simultaneously rejecting
baptismal regeneration. One such passage, Acts
19:1-7, states:

> *And it came to pass, that, while Apollos was at
> Corinth, Paul having passed through the
> upper coasts came to Ephesus: and finding
> certain disciples, he said unto them, "Have ye
> received the Holy Ghost since ye believed?"
> And they said unto him, "We have not so much
> as heard whether there be any Holy Ghost."
> And he said unto them, "Unto what then were
> ye baptized?" And they said, "Unto John's
> baptism." Then said Paul, "John verily
> baptized with the baptism of repentance, saying
> unto the people, that they should believe on him
> which should come after him, that is, on Christ
> Jesus." When they heard [this], they were
> baptized in the name of the Lord Jesus. And
> when Paul had laid [his] hands upon them, the
> Holy Ghost came on them; and they spake with*

tongues, and prophesied. And all the men were about twelve.

Second, the letter of 1 Corinthians is accepted as a doctrinal book. 1 Corinthians 1:14-17 teaches there is no correlation between baptism and salvation. Paul, under the inspiration of the Holy Spirit, stated:

> *I thank God that I baptized none of you, but Crispus and Gaius; lest any should say that I had baptized in mine own name. And I baptized also the household of Stephanas: besides, I know not whether I baptized any other. For Christ sent me not to baptize, but to preach the gospel: not with wisdom of words, lest the cross of Christ should be made of none effect.*

Paul taught that an undue emphasis on baptism could have led potentially to personality worship and divisions in the church.

Third, the choice of conjunctions in Acts 22:16 clearly contradicted a connection between baptism and the washing away of sins. "οτι," a causative word which was used in verses 2, 19, 29a, and 29b of chapter 22, was not used in verse 16. οτι means: "the reason why anything is said to be or to be done."[72] It would have been, therefore, the logical choice to demonstrate the cleansing of sin through baptism.

The conjunction chosen by the Holy Spirit, however, was "και." The configuration και . . . και, used in verse 16, was "a repetition which indicates that of two things one takes

---

[72] Carl Ludwig] Grimm and [Christian Gottlob] Wilke, Greek-English Lexicon of the New Testament, 459.

place no less than the other: both . . . and, as well . . . as, not only . . . but also."[73] Baptism and the washing away of sins, therefore, were intended to be viewed as separate activities. Saul was to be baptized and, additionally (not simultaneously), to have his sins washed away through salvation.

Fourth, the Apostle John stated in the book of John 4:1-2: "When therefore the Lord knew how the Pharisees had heard that Jesus made and baptized more disciples than John, (though Jesus himself baptized not, but his disciples)." It would appear that Jesus would have performed baptisms personally if the

---

[73] Carl Ludwig] Grimm and [Christian Gottlob] Wilke, <u>Greek-English Lexicon of the New Testament</u>, 316.

practice was necessary for salvation. He would not have left this "crucial" task to others.

This idea becomes significant when viewed in light of a statement made by Millard J. Erickson. Erickson, distinguished professor of theology at Baylor University's Truett Seminary, asserted "[There is] a . . . difficulty in using narrative passages as a basis for doctrine is the existence of apparently contradictory instances of a given doctrine."[74]

Homiletical Analysis

The seventh step of the exegetical

---

[74] Millard J. Erickson and James L. Heflin, <u>Old Wine in New Wineskins</u> (Grand Rapids: Baker Book House Co., 1997), 122.

pyramid is the homiletical analysis. Homiletics may be described as "the art and science of 'saying the same thing that the text of Scripture says.'"[75] Robert L. Thomas further clarifies this thought: "homiletics [is] the field of sermon preparation and delivery."[76]

The exposition of Acts 22:12-16 would be an example of the selective approach to homiletics. Bryson stated:

> *If an expositor preaches from a book using some: paragraphs, a few narratives, several personal choices of texts, or a number of words, no homiletical rule has been violated. The*

---

[75] Walter C. Kaiser, <u>Toward an Exegetical Theology</u> (Grand Rapids: Baker Book House Co., 1981), 193.

[76] Robert L. Thomas, "Exegesis and Expository Preaching," in <u>Rediscovering Expository Preaching</u>, ed. Richard L. Mayhue (Dallas, TX: Word Publishing Co., 1992), 144.

> *basic principle or homiletical guideline of the*
> *selective approach emphasizes flexibility and*
> *creativity.*[77]

The basic homiletical thought of Acts 22:12-16, stated previously in the "Syntactical Analysis" section (the thesis statement), is: "God appointed Saul to know His will, to see His Son, and to hear His voice so that Saul could testify on His behalf." This thesis is a particular, rather than universal, statement. The particular thesis statement thus applies only to Saul in his situation during his time.[78]

---

[77] Harold T. Bryson, <u>Expository Preaching</u>, 89.

[78] Alan Odiam, "Doctor of Ministry Seminar: Interpretation/Preaching," notebook of materials.

SERMON BRIEF

Background

Paul, in this passage, was under arrest for preaching the Gospel. God gave him the wisdom to use his circumstance to his advantage. He mentioned his Roman citizenship as leverage for allowing him to make a defense of his position. He was given the opportunity to defend his actions.

PAUL'S DEFENSE

Paul's defense, however, was simply an opportunity to share the gospel. He began to build a "bridge" using points of similarity with his Jewish audience.

Use of Native Language

First, he gained their attention by speaking in their native Hebrew language. The Jews were obviously unaware that Paul was a member of their own race.

Points of Identification

Second, Paul established several points of identification with the crowd. He discussed his background in Judaism including his studies under Gamaliel, a respected leader in the Jewish community (Acts 22:3).

Paul, like his audience, had been a zealous defender of Judaism (Acts 22:4). He, as a matter of public record, had been a chief persecutor of Christianity (Acts 22:4-5). He had already taken several Christians to prison and, at the point of his encounter with Christ, was taking others to a similar fate.

Paul's reference to Ananias said that he "was a devout man according to the law, having a good report of all the Jews which dwelt there." (Acts 22:12) Ananias, therefore, would have been readily accepted by this group of Jews.

The Basis of His Appeal

Third, he appealed to them on a "what would you have done" basis. He was blinded by a bright light, followed by a voice saying: "Saul,

Saul, why persecutest thou me?" Saul asked about the identity of the one who was addressing him, to which Jesus replied: "I am Jesus the Nazarene whom you are persecuting." Paul exercised the only logical option at this point—he asked what Jesus wanted from him and then obeyed.

Theological Considerations

Luke stated in verse 16: ". . . be baptized, and wash away thy sins." This verse has been used by another denomination to support the doctrine of "baptismal regeneration." Baptismal regeneration is the necessity of baptism for salvation.

REASONS BAPTISM IS NOT A PART OF SALVATION

There are two main arguments against the teaching that baptism is essential to the process of salvation found in Acts 22:12-16. The first argument is the choice of conjunctions used in Acts 22:16. The Holy Spirit could have included a word that means: "the reason why anything is said to be or to be done."[79] This conjunction is used in verses 2, 19, 29a, and 29b of this chapter, but was not used in verse 16. It would have been, therefore, the logical choice to validate the teaching regarding the cleansing of sin through baptism.

---

[79] Carl Ludwig] Grimm and [Christian Gottlob] Wilke, Greek-English Lexicon of the New Testament, 459.

The conjunction chosen by the Holy Spirit, "and," treats baptism and the washing away of sins as separate activities. Saul was to be baptized and, additionally (not simultaneously), to have his sins washed away through salvation.

The second argument against baptismal regeneration is that "biblical data varies in weight."[80] In other words, the rule-of-thumb is that you prefer the clear teachings of the Bible over those that are more obscure. 1 Corinthians 1:14-17 teaches:

> *I thank God that I baptized none of you, but Crispus and Gaius; lest any should say that I had baptized in mine own name. And I baptized also the household of Stephanas: besides, I know not whether I baptized any*

---

[80] Dale Ellenburg, "Doctor of Ministry Seminar: Interpretation/Preaching," notebook of materials.

other. For Christ sent me not to baptize, but to preach the gospel: not with wisdom of words, lest the cross of Christ should be made of none effect.

An undue emphasis on baptism, therefore, can potentially lead to personality worship. The relative importance of the various people who performed baptisms in a church can, ultimately, lead to divisions in the church.

The Bible also informs us in John 4:1-2: "When therefore the Lord knew how the Pharisees had heard that Jesus made and baptized more disciples than John, (though Jesus himself baptized not, but his disciples)." Jesus clearly would have performed baptisms personally if the practice was necessary for salvation. He would not have left this "crucial" task to others.

Introduction

A missions construction team was serving in Mexico during the summer of 1991. The team started work each morning at 4:00 and continued until 11:00, when the heat became unbearable. They would spend the afternoons touring the local town of Nogales. Each day would end with the team around a camp fire, studying some relevant biblical topic to their trip.

One evening, the camp leader made this statement: "The church is the entity that issues the call to a ministry. The concept of God issuing a direct call is unscriptural. God never personally 'calls' anyone to a ministry." Was he correct? No! The church may confirm a calling, but God issues the calling.

I. God Calls

A. GOD'S SELECTION OF PAUL

God personally called at least one man for ministry: the Apostle Paul. The Bible says he was "chosen" by God (verse 14). The word "chosen" means: "to take into one's hands beforehand, to plan, to purpose, to determine." This verb was used in the aorist, or point action, tense. It thus meant that God had personally selected Saul, at a definite moment in time before his conversion, for His service.

Paul further clarified this statement in Galatians 1:15-16 with the claim that he had been chosen to serve God "from . . . [his]

mother's womb." He had been selected for his salvation ministry to the Gentiles.

B. GOD'S SELECTION OF OTHERS IN THE BIBLE

The Bible mentions several other men who were similarly selected for a ministry. Samson was to be a Nazarite from birth (Judg. 13:2-25). Samuel was a servant in the temple from his childhood (1 Sam. 1:27-28). Jeremiah was chosen to be a prophet from his mother's womb (Jer. 1:5-10). John the Baptist was chosen as a forerunner to prepare the way for Jesus' ministry (Luke 1:15-17). Jesus was a chosen sacrifice from before the foundation of the world (Matt. 1:18-25; 1 Pet. 1:18-21).

II. God Equips

God not only chooses His servants, He equips them for service. Many companies hire employees based on "sink or swim." They give them very little instruction and expect them to succeed. Those who "swim" remain on, and are given additional training. Those who "sink," however, are either dismissed from employment or compensated so poorly they are forced to resign.

God did not "hire" the Apostle Paul on a "sink or swim" basis. Paul was given the following equipment to carry out his assignment: a knowledge of God's will, a revelation of God's Son, an ability to hear a word from God.

A. PAUL'S EQUIPMENT FOR SERVICE

The first piece of equipment issued to Saul was a knowledge of God's determined will for his life and the lives of others. The word "will" is the same word used in the Model Prayer (Luke 11:2), which says: "Thy will be done, as in heaven, so in earth." The Holy Spirit constantly kept Paul informed of the direction for his ministry.

Once, Paul and his companions were unclear about their next preaching assignment. They were restrained from going to several places. The Holy Spirit (Acts 16:6-10) then issued the now famous "Macedonian call" through the Apostle Paul. God, therefore, revealed His will to, and through, Paul.

The second piece of equipment was a revelation of God's Son. Paul was required to be a witness of the resurrected Jesus to qualify for the office of Apostle (Acts 1:22).

The third piece of equipment issued to Paul was the ability to hear a word from God. This was crucial for the Lord to inspire him to write more than half of the books of the New Testament.

B. OUR EQUIPMENT FOR SERVICE

God does not hire us to "sink or swim." He equips each of us to serve Him. He informs us of His will, reveals His Son to us, and speaks to us through the Bible.

God also issues spiritual gifts to each of us. We receive the spiritual gifts needed to carry out the assignments He has called us to carry out (1 Corinthians 12:1-11). These spiritual gifts are better than years of experience in the particular ministry we are called to fulfill. They are the supernatural enablement to do the task for which we have been chosen.

III. God Sends

God not only equips His servants for a ministry, but also sends them out to perform that ministry.

A. PAUL'S COMMISSIONING

God equipped Paul for a specific mission: to be His witness (Acts 22:15). He would be a witness, in the legal sense, of those things revealed to him.

Paul, like the Damascene Jews (verse 12), could be figuratively placed on the witness stand regarding those things he had seen and heard.

He was to tell "all men" about his experience with the Lord. His assignment was to inform the non-Jewish world about salvation through Jesus Christ.

B. OUR COMMISSIONING

God also commissions each of us to be a witness of those things we have seen and heard about Jesus. The "Great Commission," found in Matthew 28:18-20, applies to every believer:

> *And Jesus came and spake unto them, saying, All power is given unto me in heaven and in earth. Go ye therefore, and teach all nations, baptizing them in the name of the Father, and of the Son, and of the Holy Ghost, teaching them to observe all things whatsoever I have commanded you: and, lo, I am with you alway, even unto the end of the world. Amen.*

Invitation

Every one of you who are Christians has been called to serve the Lord in some capacity. He has equipped you to fulfill your ministry. Many of you, however, are not actively seeking to accomplish God's will for your life.

You may never have asked the Lord what He wants from you; you may have served Him in the past but, for one reason or another, are not currently serving Him; or, you may have never trusted in Jesus as Lord and Savior—you do not have a ministry because you do not have a relationship with Him. Any one of these circumstances may be true of you. If so, you need to come to the altar and give control of your life to the Lord Jesus Christ.

AILMENT THREE: ONE-SIZE-FITS-ALL[81]

Many growing Baptist churches have adopted two basic leadership models. The first, an assembly line approach to ministry, offers several benefits to a church. The method has, correspondingly, many offsetting limitations.

A second model is the team ministry approach. This method also has several strengths and counteracting weaknesses.

---

[81] This section previously included in W. Scott Moore, <u>Partners in Planting: Starting and Staffing a New Testament Church</u> (Rogersville, AL: Eleos Press, 2012), 165-191.

An alternative to both leadership models is a composite approach to ministry. This option is a blending of the best elements of both the assembly line and group ministry approaches.

ASSEMBLY LINE APPROACH

Definition and Description

The assembly line is identified as "a grouping of workers together with the machines, tools, and parts necessary to manufacture a finished product."[82] It is further characterized as an "arrangement whereby the work in process passes progressively from one operation to the next until the product is assembled."[83]

A PROCESS

An assembly line approach to ministry is, therefore, the process of taking a new believer through a series of spiritual growth steps. Members achieve the "finished product" status when they reach the goal of spiritual maturity.

---

[82] World Book Encyclopedia, 1985 ed., s.v. "Assembly Line."

[83] Microsoft Encarta Encyclopedia, 1999 ed., s.v. "Assembly Line."

Identification of Prospects

The first step in the typical assembly line process is to bring together the "raw materials" by locating lost people and leading them to faith in Jesus Christ. Soul-winning is certainly essential to the life of every church. Growing assembly line churches often perform this function remarkably well.

Addition to the Church

Second, the new converts are presented publicly to the church. They are usually allowed to receive baptism at the next service. They commonly receive little or no instruction regarding either the meaning or the procedure of baptism.

Presentation of Privileges

The newly baptized converts are granted full status as church members. They immediately acquire all associated privileges, including the right to vote in church business meetings.

Assignment to Groups

Next, the recent believers are assigned to one or more sub-groupings within the church. They are encouraged to attend age-graded classes to study the Bible. These classes are designed to serve as the infrastructures for meeting the new converts' needs for both small group Bible study and Christian fellowship.

Transition into Ministry Involvement

Fourth, at some point the new converts are usually offered opportunities to become involved in ministry. These believers are frequently viewed as having completed the growth process once they have reached this level of spiritual involvement.

ASSOCIATED STYLES OF LEADERSHIP

Church leaders generally fall into one of two main leadership categories: those that are task-oriented and those that are people-oriented. Task-oriented leaders "place . . . doing ahead of being."[84] Conversely, people-oriented leaders tend to "put . . . being ahead of doing."[85]

The former, task-orientation, is the style of leadership often associated with the assembly line model. Church leaders that adopt this approach are usually more concerned with immediate, quantifiable results (baptisms, attendance, and offerings) than with the Christian growth and development of the current membership.

---

[84] C. Peter Wagner, <u>Leading Your Church to Growth: The Secret of Pastor/People Partnership in Dynamic Church Growth</u> (Ventura, CA: Regal Books, 1984), 100.

[85] C. Peter Wagner, <u>Leading Your Church to Growth</u>, 100.

Benefits of Task-Orientation

The results-orientation style of leadership associated with an assembly line approach to ministry has one distinct benefit: the small investment necessary per convert. This benefit can be manifested in the church in several ways.

Minimal Time Investment

The first resource conservation is related to the industrial application of the assembly line—the speed of production. Many units can be assembled in a relatively short period of time.

Similarly, many new converts can be "processed" by the church in a brief interval of time. This feature is particularly helpful as a church experiences a period of rapid growth.

This concept was demonstrated through the philosophy of industrialist Henry Ford. L. Scott Bailey, publisher and president of Automobile Quarterly, stated: "Henry Ford pioneered in improving assembly line methods to cut production costs. . . . The big saving of time (emphasis added) cut Ford's production costs."[86] The discipleship process of the individual is, therefore, usually very brief.

<u>Minimal Financial Obligation</u>

The investment per unit is also necessarily lower due to the economic law of supply and demand. Increased production

---

[86] <u>World Book Encyclopedia</u>, 1985 ed., s.v. "Automobile."

costs will result in a correspondingly higher price per unit. Higher prices subsequently bring about a reduction in consumer demand. Price per unit, therefore, must be kept to a minimum to maintain the company's market position.

The investment per new convert is similarly limited. It must be confined to a percentage of the total number of assigned resources. The financial and personnel constraints of the church are necessarily reflected in the amounts that are available to be allocated to the individual believers.

Minimal Innovation Expense

The required investment per convert is also reduced because, with new Christians, there is little need for innovation. The same teachers and teaching materials can be used interchangeably with each new group of believers. Churches employing the assembly line method, consequently, Bailey validated the rationale behind this assertion by stating:

> *Basic changes in the body, engine, suspension, or transmission would be too costly to make every year. The yearly changes usually involve such relatively minor improvements as restyled fenders, radiator grilles, or tail lights.*[87]

Church leaders have discovered that they need only make minor modifications to the available resources without sacrificing the quality of personnel and materials available to their constituency.

---

[87] <u>World Book Encyclopedia</u>, 1985 ed., s.v. "Automobile."

Limitations

The assembly line approach has several inherent limitations. These deficiencies include the impersonal nature of the method, an underutilization of personnel, and an inadequate assimilation of new members.

Impersonal Nature

The first limitation is the impersonal nature of an assembly line approach. The new convert trusts Jesus through the witness of one member of the church. The ministry of the familiar church member often concludes when the new convert joins the church. Depending upon the size of the church, the two people may rarely interact.

The new convert is automatically enrolled into an existing Sunday school class. Sole responsibility for the new believer is thereby transferred to the teacher. The problem is compounded because, generally, the most effective teachers have growing classes. They are thereby limited in effectively working with their class members on an individual basis.

The more established a class becomes the greater the probability it will be composed of closed cliques within the current membership. The members of these inner circles will either see little need or have little desire to welcome the new converts.

Class leaders may attempt to remedy the situation by occasionally hosting some type of fellowship function.

These functions may have a moderate degree of success in welcoming a few of the new members into the class. They are, however, usually ineffective in making any permanent changes.

Church attendance does not guarantee that new converts will be accepted into a group. Conversations before the service are frequently discouraged, as members are expected to enter a time of personal and corporate worship.

The current members will often meet for a few moments after the service. They will discuss common areas of interest. The new members do not share the same frame of reference; they are, once again, excluded from fellowship with the group.

Inefficient Use of People Resources

A second limitation associated with the assembly line is the inefficient use of the appropriation of people resources. John G. Truxal, with reference to the automotive industry, asserted: "Many people find repetitive, simple jobs, such as working on a factory assembly line, dull and degrading."[88]   He further stated, "They have difficulty maintaining the level of interest necessary to do this type of work effectively over long periods of time."[89]

Henry Ford also found this circumstance to be true in his experience with the assembly line:

> *By early 1914 this innovation, although greatly increasing productivity, had resulted in a monthly labor turnover of 40 to 60 percent in his factory, largely because of the unpleasant monotony of assembly line work*

---

[88] World Book Encyclopedia, 1985 ed., s.v. "Automation."

[89] World Book Encyclopedia, 1985 ed., s.v. "Automation."

> *and repeated increases in the production*
> *quotas assigned to the workers.*[90]

Ambitious, successful people do not find assembly line ministries very rewarding. These people thrive on ministerial challenges. Few opportunities for meaningful service are offered through the assembly line approach to ministry.

Quality volunteers in an organization also expect recognition for a job well done. Little credit is given to those ministering productively in an assembly line environment.

Inadequate Assimilation

A third limitation may be attributed to the fact that little or no instruction is given to

---

[90] <u>Funk and Wagnall's Encyclopedia</u>, 1998 ed., s.v. "Henry Ford."

aid in their assimilation into the Christian community.

TEAM MINISTRY

A recent innovation for many churches is the "team ministry" concept. This model of church leadership also has several benefits. The model also has some offsetting limitations.

Definition and Description

A team may be defined as: "a number of persons associated together in work or activity."[91] A team ministry model, accordingly, is a group of Christians that share the ministry responsibilities of a local church.

The team ministry approach is a simple two-step process: selection of the team members and involvement in ministry. Prospects for team membership are generally limited to the current constituency of the church. Qualities such as spiritual gifts and Christian maturity help determine members' potential for productive ministries.

Second, the team members are involved in ministry. Training is involved in this step to help fulfill assigned responsibilities. This can be

---

[91] Merriam-Webster's Collegiate Dictionary, 10th edition, 1209.

accomplished both through observation of the current members of a team and by means of personal involvement.

Associated Style of Leadership

People-orientation is the style of leadership commonly found in team ministry churches. Leaders exercising this style recognize an important fact: "people must not be treated as simply means toward an end—the end or the goals must be established according to the needs of the people."[92]

---

[92] Wagner, <u>Leading Your Church to Growth</u>, 100.

BENEFITS

A people-oriented team ministry is based on the observation that the members of an organization are significant. This rationale has several resultant advantages.

Commitment to Quality

One major advantage of the team approach is an increased commitment to quality. The individual members of the group hold each other accountable for their contributions to the overall ministry process.

Quality is also ensured by the increased likelihood of team member innovation. James B. Miller, founder and Chief Executive Officer of Miller Business Systems, stated, "Employees can provide the fresh perspective and creativity they gain from interacting with customers every day."[93]

Promotion of Spiritual Growth

A second benefit of the team ministry is that it promotes the spiritual growth of church members. According to research specialist Charles Barna, "Unless the church challenge[s] the individual to develop his or her abilities, chances [are] good that the individual [will] not grow."[94] These leadership abilities can readily

---

[93] James B. Miller, <u>The Corporate Coach</u> (New York: St. Martin's Press, 1993), 82.

[94] Charles Barna, <u>User Friendly Churches: What Christians Need to Know About the Churches People Love to Go To</u> (Ventura, CA: Regal Books, 1991), 166.

be nurtured and developed in an environment of shared ministerial responsibilities.

Endurance over Time

A third benefit of the team ministry model is that the ministry has the ability to survive beyond the tenure of the current leadership group. John Maxwell is a former pastor, a motivational speaker, and the founder of INJOY Ministries. He asserted, "True success comes only when every generation continues to develop the next generation."[95]

---

[95] John Maxwell, Developing the Leaders Around You: How To Help Others Reach Their Full Potential (Nashville: Thomas Nelson Publishers, 1995), 198.

Facilitation of Relationships

A fourth benefit of the team ministry is the facilitation of interpersonal relationships within the church. These associations may facilitate the numerical growth of the congregation. According to Peter Wagner and John L. Gorsuch: "Growing churches put a higher priority on this [fellowship] than nongrowing churches."[96]

---

[96] C. Peter Wagner and Richard L. Gorsuch, "The Quality Church (Part 1)," Leadership Winter 1983, 31, quoted in John N. Vaughan, <u>The Large Church: A Twentieth-Century Expression of the First-Century Church</u> (Grand Rapids: Baker Book House, 1985), 99.

LIMITATIONS

A team ministry also has several inherent limitations. These limitations include the amount of time required for proper implementation of the ministry, the possibility of missed witnessing opportunities, and the increased potential for power struggles within the leadership core.

Time Factor

The first limitation of the team approach is the amount of time invested in the team building process. A leader's personal resources must be devoted to equipping church members to function as a team.

John Maxwell alleged, "Equipping, like nurturing, is an ongoing process. You don't equip a person in a few hours or a day. . . . Equipping must be tailored to each potential leader."[97]

Missed Opportunities

A second limitation is in the potential loss of soul-winning opportunities. The exclusive use of a team ministry method can interfere with church leaders' resources of time and energy. Leaders must demonstrate flexibility in their scheduling to meet prospects from the lost community and properly cultivate those relationships.

---

[97] Maxwell, <u>Developing the Leaders Around You</u>, 84.

Potential for Power Struggles

A team ministry approach presents a greater potential for power struggles among the church leaders. One reason for the increased capacity for disagreement is the method is not conducive to the development of a centralized power structure. A single, autocratic leader is not required to either recognize or consider the opinions of others.

Another reason for the increased potential for leader disagreement is related to the first: team ministries generally create a broader base of control. The propensity for conflict within the group is proportionate to the number of trained leaders in the local church.

A COMPOSITE MINISTRY

The implementation of a composite approach to ministry is a two-step process. The first step is to consider the five basic ministry purposes for the church. The subsequent step is to match each of the five purposes to the most appropriate ministry types for fulfillment.

Five Basic Ministry Purposes

Rick Warren, Senior Pastor of the Saddleback Valley Community Church in Orange County, California, has identified five basic purposes for the church. The descriptive words for these purposes are magnify, mission, membership, maturity, and ministry.

MAGNIFY

The first word, magnify, describes the purpose of "celebrat[ing] God's presence in worship."[98] All believers have the responsibility of worshiping God on a regular basis. They must practice this activity both corporately in the local church and individually on a more personal basis.

MISSION

Mission, as used by Warren, is "communicat[ing] God's Word through

---

[98] Rick Warren, <u>The Purpose Driven Church: Growth Without Compromising Your Message and Mission</u> (Grand Rapids: Zondervan Publishing House, 1995), 107.

evangelism."[99]   Leaders must incorporate the element of evangelism if they want their churches to reach people and grow numerically.

MEMBERSHIP

The third descriptive word to describe the purpose of the church is membership. Membership is defined as the "incorporat[ion of] God's family into . . . [the] fellowship . . . [of a church]."[100]

---

[99] Ibid., 107.

[100] Ibid., 107.

MATURITY

Maturity is "educat[ing] God's people through discipleship."[101] Churches should be the primary agents for assisting believers in spiritual growth.

MINISTRY

Rick Warren stated that the church has the responsibility to "demonstrate God's love through service."[102] All believers are called to perform some facet of a personal ministry as representatives of the local church.

---

[101] Rick Warren, <u>The Purpose Driven </u>Church, 107.

[102] Ibid., 107.

Most Appropriate Ministry Types

The assembly line method, based upon its unique strengths, is the best choice for fulfilling the purposes of evangelism and assimilation of members. Conversely, utilization of the team ministry approach is more advantageous in fulfilling the purposes of worship, discipleship, and Christian service.

EVANGELISM AND ASSIMILATION

The assembly line model is especially suited for handling the entry stages of church membership. These stages include the purposes of "mission" (evangelism) and "membership" (assimilation).

Evangelism

First, the evangelistic efforts of a church can be managed through an assembly line approach. The process of conversion is one that does not require constant revision.

Most church members can be trained in soul-winning methodologies. They can distribute and explain gospel tracts with prospects. These members are also capable of learning and sharing a simple plan of salvation, such as the "Romans Road."[103]

---

[103] Romans 3:23, 6:23, 5:8, 10:9, 10:10, and 10:13.

Assimilation

Second, follow-up of converts ("assimilation") can be handled successfully through the assembly line method. All new believers can be given an identical explanation of the need for baptism and church membership.

The assembly line method can also accommodate new believers' classes. The basic tenets of the Christian life can be explained by means of an ongoing class structure. The assembly line is also useful in acclimating new church members. A standard class can be formed to explain the unique belief structures and characteristics of the church.

Worship, Discipleship, and Christian Service

The team ministry model is especially appropriate for dealing with the three developmental stages of church membership. First, a ministry team could be constructed to assist in the purpose of worship ("magnify"). Second, a ministry team can more effectively handle the discipleship ("maturity") aspects of the church. Third, a ministry team could be assigned the service ("ministry") functions of the congregation.

Worship

The members of a worship team could coordinate the efforts of several segments within the local church to produce a more effective overall ministry that honors the Lord. One segment of the worship team could focus on the overall atmosphere of the church during the various services throughout the week. They could assist in such factors as preliminary prayer, planning the orders of service, and decoration of the sanctuary.

Another segment of the worship team could focus on age-graded choirs. A subgroup working with the children's choirs would consist of several members that recognize the importance of teaching children to worship the Lord at an early age. Those that assist the teenagers might focus on instructing them in a greater understanding of the concept of properly praising the Lord. Another segment would be responsible for working with the adult choirs.

Additional workers could prepare for each service through prayer. They could also establish teams to pray for peoples' needs during the services.

Discipleship

A team can competently facilitate the spiritual growth of church members. The team approach can be used successfully for at least two fundamental reasons: a smaller teacher-disciple ratio and greater accountability.

Smaller Teacher-Disciple Ratio

First, a smaller teacher-disciple ratio allows for more personal time with each convert. This arrangement can be beneficial to both the disciples and the teachers.

The disciples benefit from the exchange because they are personally challenged to follow through with the discipleship exercises. They also have more latitude in interaction with their teachers—obtaining answers that will assist them in understanding the concepts presented. Additionally, disciples in small group situations are more likely allowed the privilege of observing their teachers' responses to real-life situations.

The teachers also profit from the arrangement. Jesus stated a principle in Mark 8:35: "For whosoever will save his life shall lose it; but whosoever shall lose his life for my sake and the gospel's, the same shall save it." Counselor Les Carter and businessman Jim Underwood likewise observed: "people can find their own significance by actively touching the lives of others."[104]

<u>Team Member Accountability</u>

The assignment of discipleship responsibilities to a team automatically increases the obligation of the members. Each can hold the others accountable for such items as curriculum selection, lesson preparation, and group member follow-up.

<u>Service</u>

Third, a ministry team would be the proper choice to perform and coordinate the service responsibilities assigned to the

---

[104] Les Carter and Jim Underwood, <u>The Significance Principle: The Secret Behind High Performance People and Organizations</u> (Nashville: Broadman and Holman Publishers, 1998), 198.

church. A team is needed to perform ministry functions because of the direction given by the Apostle Paul in 1 Corinthians 12:4-7:

> *Now there are diversities of gifts, but the Same Spirit. And there are differences of administrations, but the same Lord. And there are diversities of operations, but it is the same God which worketh all in all. But the manifestation of the Spirit is given to every man to profit withal.*

A team can also be helpful in establishing a suitable framework for ministry. Team members can work together in certain ministries, assist one another in accountability needs, and form a council to provide the necessary leadership to properly carry out each ministry objective.

CONCLUSION

Most churches have consciously, or unconsciously, adopted either the assembly line method or the team ministry approach. A church can effectively minister using either program.

The most effective churches will first pray for guidance. They will then select the best possible combination of the two.

A composite ministry method can be infinitely variable. The leadership of the church can best determine the purposes that should be fulfilled through the assembly line or as a team. Individual purposes can also be accomplished through a mixture of the two.

The greatest need, therefore, is to examine the church and make the choice.

Traditional patterns cannot be perpetuated simply because they are uncomplicated.

The church is obligated to perform a ministry at its highest possible level. The composite ministry is one of many tools that can assist in reaching this primary goal.

AILMENT FOUR: STAGNATION

A second morning worship service can be an invaluable tool for the growth of a local church. These services have contributed to both the numerical and financial growth of many churches of various sizes. They have also been effective in reaching new people with the gospel of Jesus Christ.

Church leaders who would establish such a program should examine the advantages of offering an additional worship service. They should, conversely, investigate and be prepared to handle the potential objections that might be associated with the service. The leaders should then anticipate, and be equipped to manage, the details associated with an additional service. Finally, the services should be periodically assessed to monitor their effectiveness in fulfilling the stated objectives.

ADVANTAGES

The advantages for multiple morning worship services are manifold. Multiple morning worship services use the church facilities more effectively. They allow more people to become involved in a ministry. These services communicate concern for the unchurched and the church members. They can benefit those involved in leading both services.

More Efficient Employment of Facilities

The first advantage is that multiple services provide a more efficient employment of church facilities. Architect and church consultant Ray Bowman asserted, "Until a church fully utilizes its existing building, a need for more space does not exist."[105]

Moulton Baptist Church in Moulton, Alabama began a dual morning service format thirteen years ago under the leadership of Dr. Darryl Wood. This pastor claimed that a second worship service not only "doubles seating space,

---

[105] Ray Bowman and Eddy Hall, <u>When Not to Build: An Architect's Unconventional Wisdom for the Growing Church</u> (Grand Rapids: Baker Book House, 1992), 58.

[but also] doubles parking space."[106] He quoted the widely accepted statistic that "when seating is at 80 percent of capacity, attendance adjusts accordingly."[107] This can, therefore, be quite advantageous to a church that has currently outgrown its available meeting space.

A multiple morning worship service can be invaluable even if current space is sufficient. A single morning worship service underutilizes a church building during a prime time when people could attend. No facility designed to reach people for Jesus should ever be underemployed.

---

[106] W. Scott Moore, "Multiple Morning Worship Service Questionnaire" (Moulton, AL: Pleasant Grove Baptist Church, 1998), 1, photocopied.

[107] Ibid., 1.

More People Involved

Second, having multiple services will necessarily multiply the number of people involved in ministry. According to John C. Maxwell, president of INJOY Ministries, the most important person in a church service (after the guest) is the usher. He claimed:

> *The ushers are important because they are often the ones who have the first contact with people. They help people with directions. They are the ones who represent the church to newcomers. They maintain order in the church service, enabling it to flow smoothly.*[108]

---

[108] John C. Maxwell, Ushers and Greeters (El Cajon, CA: INJOY Ministries, 1991), 1-5; quoted in Gary L. McIntosh, The Exodus Principle: A Five-Part Strategy to Free Your People for Ministry (Nashville: Broadman and Holman Publishers, 1995), 155.

Unless the current staff of ushers is already doing all of the above-named tasks, these new ushers should be trained by someone other than the current director. This person should have a desire to reach people through the additional service. This director should share the vision for the type of ministry needed to successfully lead in this service.

Maxwell further said that the next person in order of importance in a worship service is the nursery worker. Nursery workers:

> *are vital because young parents will select a church more on the nursery care than on the doctrinal statements of the congregation. Nursery workers give assurance to the parents that their child will be cared for.[109]*

---

[109] Maxwell, Ushers and Greeters, 155.

Additional nursery workers will be needed to take care of the children of those attending the new worship service. A separate nursery coordinator working under the direction of the current coordinator will also be extremely helpful.

Another necessary group includes "the worship leader and the people who sing."[110] This could involve the same people as the current service. The service will also, however, conceivably incorporate new people in positions of leadership and special performances.

Counselors are also needed to speak with those who are making decisions. These

---

[110] Ibid., 156.

counselors should be individually paired with those making decisions. They should then escort the counselees to a counseling room. The counselors are thus enabled to give them the personalized attention and to simplify the flow of people between worship services. Any decisions can be shared with the members at the conclusion of a future worship service.

Expresses Concern for the Needs of People

Third, the presence of multiple services expresses concern for the needs of people. Merchants in the marketplace have learned that business hours should be set at the customer's convenience. People will gravitate to those businesses that are open when they want to shop. The churches that are "open for business" when people are ready to go will have, obviously, more "customers" than those who do not. According to the senior pastor of the Mecklenburg Community Church in Charlotte, North Carolina: "Most persons do not want their day disrupted to the degree that a service ending at noon has the tendency to accomplish."[111] Jim McCoy, Minister of Music in a church that has offered multiple morning worship services for years, stated: "we were able to reach some people who were looking for a church that offered an early service."[112]

---

[111] James Emery White, <u>Opening the Front Door: Worship and Church Growth</u> (Nashville: Convention Press, 1992), 102.

[112] Moore, "Worship Service Questionnaire," 1.

Flexibility, however, should not be confused with accommodation. According to an exhaustive study of 576 evangelistic churches, "accommodation means that the church has let the world dictate its standards. The gospel is no longer authoritative; all authority resides in culture."[113] The delicate "balance [is] between separation and accommodation."[114] The gospel should be accessible without diminishing its message.

Multiple morning services can also meet church member needs. Jim McCoy initially felt that an early service was a concession until he

---

[113] Thom Rainer, Effective Evangelistic Churches (Nashville: Broadman and Holman Publishers, 1996), 47.

[114] Laney L. Johnson, The Church: God's People on Mission (Nashville: Convention Press, 1995), 91.

observed the commitment level of the people attending. He stated he then realized: "people are not looking for just convenience—they just want to get started a little earlier."[115] Darryl Wood concurred: "the additional service is helpful to folks who have an obligation later in the day; [the] option helps meet busy schedules."[116]

Another advantage to church members is that the two services will differ in size. One service will have more in attendance than the other. Wood stated that this attendance differential benefits "people who prefer smaller numbers [the] opportunity [to worship with a

---

[115] Moore, "Worship Service Questionnaire," 1.

[116] Moore, "Worship Service Questionnaire," 1.

smaller group]. Some folks prefer the smaller church atmosphere."[117]

Beneficial to Those Leading Services

Multiple services can be beneficial to those involved in leading both services. The greatest benefit is that the early service gives the leader occasion to fine tune the second service. Dr. Wood said that the preacher "get[s] two tries to get the sermon right."[118]

The musicians also benefit from the additional service. Musician Jim McCoy uses

---

[117] Ibid., 1.

[118] Moore, "Worship Service Questionnaire," 1.

the same soloist in both morning services. He claimed the first service can be a "trial run. [It] gives the soloist a chance to sing in front of a smaller group. [It is an opportunity to take care of any] glitches in the service."[119]

POTENTIAL OBJECTIONS

Several potential objections may arise when initiating multiple services. These objections can be avoided if handled properly. Objections should be anticipated and dealt with before the presentation of the proposal to the church.

---

[119] Ibid., 1.

Dr. Darryl Wood stated one objection is the belief that the new service can "hurt [the] fellowship [of the church]."[120] Some people believe an additional service can create a group of church members with whom they will never fellowship. Members of large churches with a single worship service express this sentiment. They are simply afraid of, or against, the growth of the church.

Some people desire to keep the church from growing to maintain their status. More people would, necessarily, give them less control and recognition in the life of the church.

Another reason some oppose growth is they avoid associating with new people. They

---

[120] Moore, "Worship Service Questionnaire," 2.

either fear these "strangers" or are unwilling to make the effort to befriend others.

This objection can be dealt with by pointing out that Jesus wants the church to minister to more people. The comfort of the current membership is secondary to the directive of the "Great Commission." The obedient church does not have the luxury of a maintenance mentality, but rather strive for growth through evangelistic outreach.

A second objection is that the additional service will require "too much work."[121] This objection is legitimate, and will likely come from those serving in a leadership capacity. The addition of a second service will require more

---

[121] Moore, "Worship Service Questionnaire," 2.

work than a single service. Church leaders, however, should not focus on the problems. They should emphasize the potential to more fully use facility and personnel resources.

A third criticism of initiating an additional worship service is "not enough people will attend to make it worthwhile."[122] This objection can be handled easily by offering to start the service on a trial basis. The new service will be continued only if enough people support it through their attendance.

Four additional objections are enumerated in a Metropolitan Life sales training manual. The writer asserted, "There are four

------

[122] Ibid., 2.

types of objections."[123] The first objection is "no confidence."

> *No confidence . . . may be expressed as a lack of confidence in you. . . . To overcome this negativism you must be positive in the use of your references, your appearance, approach, manner, knowledge, enthusiasm, etc.*[124]

The entire process of starting a new worship service should be, therefore, clearly spelled out before presenting the proposal to the church.

The support of key leaders must also be solicited in advance to enlist their endorsement. People will naturally follow these leaders. They

---

[123] Professional Sales Development—Phase I: You and Your Family (U.S.A.: Metropolitan Life Insurance Company, 1976), 27.

[124] Ibid., 27.

are extremely interested in leaders' opinions regarding any new program offered by the church.

The second objection is "no want." The church members may simply not want to have an additional worship service. A remedy for this objection is to "show that there is a need and a want. Fix the problem."[125] One need that can be met by multiple worship services is the provision of adequate space to meet the demands of a growing congregation. People are frequently unwilling to attend a church service that is consistently overcrowded.

An additional need that can be addressed by multiple worship services is the incorporation

---

[125] Professional Sales Development, 27.

of a segment of the local community unreached by the current worship structures. Many people have conflicts such as work schedules and family commitments and simply cannot attend the existing service. An alternate worship time can be an encouragement to them to attend.

Another need may be poor stewardship of available resources. The existing structure should be used to its maximum capacity. This is a viable consideration even if current space is adequate to meet the current demands of the present congregation.

The third basic objection is "no money." The church members "may say, '[we] . . . can't afford it.'"[126] They may thus be concerned

---

[126] Professional Sales Development, 27.

W. Scott Moore

about the increased cost of utilities and other expenses associated with the additional service. This objection will likely come from a "critic [that] does not trust in a supernatural God with abundant resources."[127] It is best handled by explaining the fact that the souls are, ultimately, more important than the money that would have to be invested to reach them. New people will also eventually bring in more revenue.

The final objection is "no hurry." Church members may agree that the additional service would be beneficial, but respond: "there's no rush about this. [Talk to us about this] next year." [128]A time of prayerful

---

[127] Rainer, <u>Effective Evangelistic Churches</u>, 155.

[128] <u>Professional Sales Development</u>, 27.

consideration is definitely warranted, but this objection need not delay progress. There are people the church can reach today who may be unreachable a year from now. Some will have moved away from the community. Others will have lost their ability to understand the gospel due to some illness or physical trauma. Others will simply have died. God is a God of the present time, the "I am" of the Bible (Ex. 3:14). His timetable for reaching people is, therefore, continuously today (2 Corinthians 6:2). Church members must be willing to do today whatever they can to reach people.

MANAGING THE DETAILS

Several steps are necessary in the planning and implementation phase of an additional worship service. Ministry teams must be recruited and properly trained; the new service must be promoted and advertised; and the increased flow of people to and from worship services must be coordinated.

Ministry Teams

The first step in preparation for a new worship service is recruiting and training a ministry team. The success of the new venture will largely depend upon finding the right people.

RECRUITING A MINISTRY TEAM

God wants the church to choose the best qualified laborers to begin a new work. John

Maxwell, an authority on the subject of church leadership, maintained that church leaders should: "look inside as well as outside the organization to find candidates."[129] Maxwell's plan, which he called the "Five A's" included: assessment of needs, assets on hand, ability of candidates, attitude of candidates, and accomplishments of candidates.[130]

Three steps in the selection of ministry team candidates can be taken from four of Maxwell's "Five A's." The first step in candidate selection should be an "assessment of needs." Maxwell simply asked the question, "what is

---

[129] Maxwell, <u>Developing the Leaders Around You</u>, 39.

[130] Ibid., 39.

needed?"[131] These needs should be written as job descriptions. Each aspect of a particular ministry team function needs to be clearly outlined.

The second (and perhaps most crucial) step eliminates those who are reluctant to serve. The question John Maxwell asked in this "attitude of candidates" section was "who is willing?"[132] Motivational speaker and author Zig Ziglar recognized the universality of agreement regarding the importance of a potential candidate's attitudes. He stated that everyone "share[s] the opinion that [a person's] attitude . . . [in] undertak[ing] a project is the dominant

---

[131] Maxwell, <u>Developing the Leaders Around You</u>, 39.

[132] Ibid., 39.

factor in its success."[133] Ziglar further asserted, "A positive attitude will have positive results because attitudes are contagious."[134] Dr. Edwin F. Jenkins, former Director of Leadership and Church Growth for the Alabama Baptist State Convention, concurred: "Most persons agree in the value of one's attitude to help or hinder, to lift or lower one's approach and accomplishment in life's pursuits."[135]

Inexperienced workers requiring job training would, consequently, be preferable to skilled workers.

---

[133] Ziglar, <u>See You at the Top</u>, 202.

[134] Ibid., 210.

[135] Edwin F. Jenkins, "The Altitude of Church Growth: An Issue of Attitude or Aptitude?," <u>The Alabama Baptist</u>, 30 April 1998, p. 8.

The third step combines the second and fifth "A's:" "assets on hand" and the "accomplishments of candidates." Two questions that should be asked are "who are the people already in the organization who are available?" and "who gets things done?"[136] Those who have already distinguished themselves in the performance of a similar task should be approached. The details should be delineated to ensure the willingness of the potential leaders to fulfill the requirements peculiar to the new service.

The right people can be placed in the right positions of responsibility once these

---

[136] Maxwell, <u>Developing the Leaders Around You</u>, 39.

questions have been answered. This will produce several benefits:

> *maximized natural energy; reduced anxiety, conflict, and tension; increased productivity; increased team spirit, morale, and respect; improved communication; increased confidence; and increased efficiency and competitiveness.*[137]

TRAINING A MINISTRY TEAM

The training process for team members should begin in the classroom. An expert in the field could be enlisted to lead the class personally or to lead the class by means of a

---

[137] Bobb Biehl, <u>Stop Setting Goals If You Would Rather Solve Problems</u> (Nashville: Moorings, Random House, Inc., 1995), 66.

series of videotapes. This classroom experience can be helpful in making the transition from the ministry pattern already established in the current worship service.

The classroom is only the beginning of the training process. Doug Fields, Youth Pastor at Saddleback Church, listed several steps that can be useful in the educational process. First, team members need to be assigned "specific responsibilities that have meaning and purpose."[138] People are not interested in becoming involved in ministries that *anyone* [emphasis added] can do. They want to be challenged to do something of lasting value that

---

[138] Doug Fields, <u>Purpose Driven Youth Ministry: Nine Essential Foundations for Healthy Growth</u> (Grand Rapids: Zondervan Publishing House, 1998), 298.

is a significant contribution to the Kingdom of God.

Second, expectations for team members should be "continually communicate[d]."[139] He further emphasized this point by stating: "Leaders won't mind hearing your expectations, but they will mind being held accountable for things they haven't been told."[140] Repetition of ministry requirements is a crucial step because a breakdown in the communication process can weaken the relationship between team members. It can also affect, ultimately, the flow of the worship services.

---

[139] Fields, <u>Purpose Driven Youth Ministry</u>, 301.

[140] Ibid., 301.

Another step Fields mentioned was "find out how your leaders are ministering."[141] This is a time for response from the team members. They can be praised for their accomplishments in fulfilling their ministry functions. Potential problems can be solved before becoming serious obstacles to the ministry.

A fourth step is to "provide the [outstanding team members] with more pastoral responsibilities."[142] People become complacent and experience boredom when doing repetitive tasks. They need to be challenged to grow by taking on new and greater ministry responsibilities in the worship service. This not

---

[141] Fields, <u>Purpose Driven Youth Ministry</u>, 304.

[142] Ibid., 304.

only fulfills the needs of team members to make significant contributions, but also increases the probability of keeping them in their current positions of service.

Fifth, the growth and development of these leaders can be encouraged by "put[ting] them over a team of other leaders."[143] This will also have the added benefit of exposing the new leaders be to the wisdom and experience of the more mature leaders.

Finally, "burdenless staff meetings" need to be designed.[144] This objective can be accomplished primarily by focusing on spiritual victories and goals the members are striving to

---

[143] Fields, <u>Purpose Driven Youth Ministry</u>, 306.

[144] Ibid., 307.

achieve. "Business issues [should be avoided because they can be] discussed and decisions . . . made during the course of any given day."[145] These issues should also be avoided due to their inability to inspire motivation from the members of the team.

PROMOTION AND ADVERTISEMENT

The new service, to successfully reach people, must be adequately promoted. Several means of promotion are available to the church. Gary L. McIntosh, associate professor and director of the doctor of ministry program at

---

[145] Fields, <u>Purpose Driven Youth Ministry</u>, 308.

the Talbot School of Theology in LaMirada California, asserted: "word of mouth . . . [is] the most effective way of advertising any organization—even a church."[146] "Word of mouth" will be, obviously, more effective if the present church members are convinced of the need for, and the value of, the new service.

"Word of mouth" will become a more significant factor after the new service is in place. It "is not based on one thing you do or don't do. It's the result of tens or hundreds of little things you do consistently well."[147] The service must be of the highest quality to both

---

[146] Gary L. McIntosh, The Exodus Principle: A 5-Part Strategy to Free Your People for Ministry (Nashville: Broadman and Holman Publishers, 1995), 101.

[147] Ibid., 103.

silence the critics and build confidence in the supporters. The reports concerning the new service will be positive and growth will likely follow.

A second means of promotion is the use of advertising. Advertising is simply "letting people know that your church is ready to serve them is vital to attracting new guests."[148] Advertising can include such things as a promotional brochure, a telephone book or newspaper ad, and the use of radio and television commercials.

A promotional brochure can also be called "A First Impression Piece."[149] It should

---

[148] McIntosh, <u>The Exodus Principle</u>, 117.

[149] Ibid., 124.

either be initially written, or revised, to include details of the new worship service.

The telephone book ad is similar to the promotional brochure. The ad should either be drafted or revised to notify the public of the new service.

The use of other media, including newspaper ads and radio and television commercials, should focus primarily on the additional morning worship time. People respond more favorably to institutions that maintain the flow of information regarding any significant organizational changes and plans for the future.

W. Scott Moore

COORDINATION OF THE FLOW OF PEOPLE

Two basic traffic flow problems are associated with beginning a new worship service. One such matter is the flow of traffic within the church facility. One major consideration is the foyer. Architect Ray Bowman suggested the use of something he described as:

> *A fellowship foyer. . . . [This foyer] is large enough to give worshipers leaving one service and those arriving for the next enough room to visit with each other and welcome visitors without blocking traffic.[150]*

---

[150] Bowman and Hall, <u>When Not to Build</u>, 123.

Another design consideration that can aid in people management is greater accessibility of areas of potentially high traffic. Rooms such as the nursery and greeting stations should be placed in convenient locations. They should be near the sanctuary with hallways large enough to accommodate the volume of people during the transition between services.

Ministry team members can also be indispensable in the movement of people throughout the facility. The ushers and greeters and welcome committee members can help the newcomers navigate through the church buildings. The counselors can help make room for those coming to the later service by directing those making decisions in the early service to another location.

The other traffic flow problem is the movement into, and out of, the parking lot. Parking is such a crucial matter that Kennon L. Callahan, founder and senior consultant of the National Institute for Church Planting and Consultation, stated:

> *Some researchers suggest that it is important for a church to have approximately 20 percent of its parking area empty on a given Sunday so that the large hidden sign that is hung out front says "come on in; there is room in the inn for you."*[151]

---

[151] Kennon L. Callahan, Twelve Keys to an Effective Church: Strategic Planning for Mission (San Francisco, CA: HarperSanFrancisco, Harper Collins Publishers, 1983), 89.

People coming to the late service must find a parking place or they will develop an unfavorable opinion regarding the early service.

ASSESSMENT OF THE SERVICE

The new service must be assessed regularly to find its effectiveness in meeting goals. The instruments of assessment can be either formal or informal. Formal instruments could include such things as questionnaires, surveys, and response forms.

Informal means could also be used in the assessment of the additional service. This category could include meetings conducted in either a personal or group setting.

CONCLUSION

Two elements are crucial to the success of a second worship service. First, God's direction must be sought in the matter. No venture should be attempted without His leadership. Jesus said in John 15:5: "Without me ye can do nothing." No plan that ignores Jesus' counsel will be fruitful.

The other crucial element is the church's leadership structure. George Barna claimed: "The church must have a leader supported by a team of people who have complementary gifts."[152] He further asserted, "Effective

---

[152] "Effective Churches: Barna Reveals Church Habits Necessary for Greater Effectiveness in Ministry," The Alabama Baptist, 7 May 1998, p. 9.

churches build their structures around such a team approach to ministry."[153] This leadership team, in submission to the Lord and with the support of the membership, can make an effective transition to a multiple worship service arrangement.

---

[153] Ibid., 9.

AILMENT FIVE: TOLERANCE TOWARD SIN

Pastors, by virtue of their involvement in a helping profession, must deal with people's needs on a personal and a corporate basis. Counseling, therefore, is a necessary function for every pastor.

One area of counseling, often overlooked as a subclassification, is church discipline. Church discipline is not a manmade system, but a biblical concept. Several reasons exist as to why it should be exercised in the church. Discipline is extremely valuable in the life of a church, and may be used as a model of pastoral counseling.

People respond in different ways to discipline. Problems are, consequently, associated with the process. These problems, however, can frequently be eliminated when certain guidelines are followed.

A BIBLICAL CONCEPT

The term "church discipline" (like the terms "Trinity" and "rapture") is not found in the Bible. The idea, however, is definitely taught.

The clearest definition etymologically is found in 2 Corinthians 2:6. The word used is επιτιμια, a noun form that occurs only once in the Greek New Testament. Επιτιμια is used only once, and translated "punishment" in the King James Version of the Bible.[154]

The verb form, επιτιμαω, occurs twenty-nine times in the Greek New Testament, and is translated as rebuke (twenty-four times), charge (four times), and straightly charge (once).[155] The word is a compound word—a combination of the two words επι and τιμη. Επι, in this usage, refers metaphorically to "that upon which any action, effect, condition, rests as a basis or support, or upon the ground of."[156]

---

[154] J. B. Smith, Greek-English Concordance to the New Testament (Scottsdale, PA: Mennonite Publishing House, 1955), 146.

[155] Ibid., 146.

[156] Thayer, Greek-English Lexicon of the New Testament, 232.

Τιμη means: "a valuing by which the price is fixed."[157] Τιμη, in turn, comes from the root word tiw, which is translated: "to estimate or to honor."[158]

The joint word, therefore, means: "to award honor or blame."[159] The process of discipline is a means of appraising a Christian's life to award the commensurate honor or blame.

Second Corinthians 2:6 refers to the following situation described by Paul in 1

---

[157] Friedrich, <u>Theological Dictionary of the New Testament</u>, vol. 8, 169.

[158] Thayer, <u>Greek-English Lexicon of the New Testament</u>, 624.

[159] Friedrich, Theological Dictionary of the New Testament, vol. 8, 169.

Corinthians 5:1-5:

> *It is reported commonly that there is fornication among you, and such fornication as is not so much as named among the Gentiles, that one should have his father's wife. And ye are puffed up, and have not rather mourned, that he that hath done this deed might be taken away from among you. For I verily, as absent in body, but present in spirit, have judged already, as though I were present, concerning him that hath so done this deed, in the name of our Lord Jesus Christ, when ye are gathered together, and my spirit, with the power of our Lord Jesus Christ, to deliver such an one unto Satan for the destruction of the flesh, that the spirit may be saved in the day of the Lord Jesus.*

The idea, then, is that a valuation should be made of the activities of those who are members of the church. This is in keeping with Jesus' teachings in Matthew 7:20: "Wherefore by their fruits ye shall know them." Actions of church members will eventually demonstrate their true relationship to the Lord. Once their activities are evaluated as sinful, action should be taken.

REASONS FOR CHURCH DISCIPLINE

Jeff Noblit, pastor of First Baptist Church in Muscle Shoals, Alabama, believes there are twelve benefits associated with exercise of church discipline. They are:

> *to glorify God by obedience to His instructions [,] . . . to restore repentant believers[,] . . . to sanctify the Lord's Supper[,] . . . to purify the spirit and message of the church[,] . . . to deny Satan any advantage in the church[,] . . . to prove that leaders love and care[,] . . . to deter others from sin[,] . . . to destroy fleshly lusts in a believer[,] . . . to Cut emotional ties with*

*unrepentant Christians[,] . . . to protect
Scripture from perversion and error[,] . . . to
shame a brother to repentance[, and] . . . to
purge out unregenerate Church members.*[160]

Three of these reasons have particular merit: to deny Satan an advantage in the church, to deter others from sin, and to protect scripture from perversion and error. Two additional reasons, to maintain the authority structure of the church and to provide a support network for overcoming the sin, are also worthy of consideration.

---

[160] Jeff Noblit, "The Principle of Church Discipline," audiotape of a sermon presented at First Baptist Church, Muscle Shoals, AL, 1997.

W. Scott Moore

Denies Satan an Advantage in the Church

Satan is always looking for ways to infiltrate the church and destroy its effectiveness. Noblit taught:

> *2 Corinthians 2:11 [says that] in the context of church discipline . . . when you practice church discipline in essence, you are defeating Satan's schemes.*[161]

Satan will use unchallenged sin in a church member's life in two primary ways. First, he will use it to damage the church's credibility in the community. The type of sin mentioned in 1 Corinthians 5 was so unusual

---

[161] Noblit, "The Principle of Church Discipline," audiotape.

that it was completely unheard of in the lost community. Satan was able to use the presence of this sin to offend the community with the ungodliness of the church.

Second, Satan destroys churches primarily from within. God has commanded that His people be holy (1 Peter 1:16). The devil weakens the church and its relationship with the Lord through an attack on its holiness.

He also destroys the foundation of the church when some members tolerate sin and others want to address it. The church is left in a state of disunity; it becomes divided regarding its purpose for existence.

Deters Others from Sin

Church discipline is necessary when a Christian either is currently involved in or planning to engage in a dangerous or questionable activity. Discipline is essential because of sin's devastating effects both on the lives of individual members and on the church as a whole. Noblit declared:

> *1 Timothy 5:20 says [that] when an elder or a church leader in general is in sin, and they don't get it right, then you are to rebuke them publicly that the rest may be fearful of sinning.*[162]

---

[162] Noblit, "The Principle of Church Discipline," audiotape.

A sin that is not confronted eventually produces a level of tolerance for ungodly behavior in the church. Some, as a result, will participate in the same or similar sin. Others may not personally become involved in a particular sin but, because it has been unchallenged, begin to condone the offense in the lives of others.

The sin must, therefore, be exposed to arrest its effects on the church. The individual's and the church's welfare are at stake.

Protects Scripture from Perversion and Error

Sin that is not challenged consequently leads to an acceptance of doctrinal error.

Acceptance of sin can also lead to a rejection of the scriptures as the basis for daily living.

Jeff Noblit taught: "This is church discipline that would deal specifically with a false teacher."[163]   Discipline of false teachers is necessary because many Christians can be led to believe the Bible is culturally biased and ultimately consider the Bible to be totally irrelevant.

People equate the church's unofficial position regarding a particular sin as synonymous with God's position.   A commitment to the authority of God's Word,

---

[163] Noblit, "The Principle of Church Discipline," audiotape.

therefore, must be maintained in the local church.

Church discipline shows that God does not lower His standard to deal with sin. He gives Christians the grace to live up to His established pattern.

Maintains the Authority Structure of the Church

Church discipline also helps to maintain an authority structure in the church. God has personally affirmed the process of discipline, as displayed in the Old Testament example of the sons of Korah (found in Numbers 16). He validated Moses' leadership position, and displayed His ultimate control over the administration of His people.

The familiar example of Ananias and Sapphira, found in Acts 5:13, illustrates the result of church discipline: "And of the rest durst no man join himself to them: but the people magnified them." The people recognized that the apostles were not to be taken lightly, and that they should be respected for their positions within the church.

A great demonstration that the Lord has instituted church discipline for the preservation of church leadership is mentioned in Acts 5:14. The Bible continues: "And believers were the more added to the Lord, multitudes both of men and women." The gospel was effectively presented as the church members' renewed respect for godly authority increased.

Provides a Support Network

Another reason for correcting behavior in the church is the potential for providing a good support network. A support network may be defined as one or more people:

> *who won't be frustrated by our slow progress, and who won't give us quick and easy solutions. . . . This person can listen to us reflectively instead of lecturing us and making judgmental statements about what we say. . . . [They are] a person or group of persons with whom you can be open and honest, who objectively can listen to you and share with you, and who will encourage you to make real, rather than surface, progress.*[164]

---

[164] Robert S. McGee, The Search for Significance (Nashville: Lifeway Press, 1992), 30.

A network is, essentially, a group of caring Christians who can help repentant believers in the process of restoration.

WHY A SUPPORT NETWORK IS NEEDED

Christians have weaknesses, personal levels of trauma, and character flaws that have influenced them to live ungodly lives. They are often unable to perceive the resultant damage from sin until it is much too late. They need "to spot trouble early on and make a course correction before a problem develops."[165]

---

[165] Robert Hemfelt, Frank Minirth, and Paul Meier, <u>Love is a Choice</u> (Nashville: Thomas Nelson Publishers, 1989), 260

First, believers may fear the destruction of their relational support networks. Their sins, once known to family members and close friends, could damage the trust upon which those relationships are built. These Christians must keep them hidden in order to preserve their associations.

Second, they may have allowed unrecognized sins to develop into patterns of behavior. These patterns are so ingrained that they produce serious errors in judgment. These believers are unable to help themselves, and need the assistance of others in the Christian community.

Third, the consequences of their sins may have produced some form of severe depression. This imbalance can affect their Christian faith and, ultimately, their total well-being. They need the external perspectives of godly people to be restored to emotional health.

WHY CHRISTIANS LACK NETWORKS

Many Christians do not have a support network for two basic reasons. The first is disobedience of the parts of other Christians. The Bible tells us in Galatians 6:2: "Bear ye one another's burdens, and so fulfil the law of Christ." They are unwilling, for some reason, to give their time to those who are hurting.

The other, more common reason, is that hurting Christians will not allow anyone to see their pain. They have attempted to reveal their sins to others in the past, and have been disappointed by the response. These Christians are now determined to handle their difficulties themselves.

BUILDING A SUPPORT NETWORK

Christians must remember the admonition given in Ecclesiastes. 4:9-12 as they seek to identify and add people to their networks. Two people working together are better than one and three are better than two. They should, therefore, share the truth about hidden sins in their past lives with two or more people whom they trust.

The Holy Spirit is the greatest member of Christian networks. He is the supreme comforter and encourager. According to restored Christian Gordon McDonald:

> *The grace to rebuild first came from God. It was there all the time for the asking, ever since the cross guaranteed its availability to anyone who sincerely asked. The challenge for me was in receiving it appropriately.*[166]

Believers in Jesus Christ have access to His personal involvement in their lives. He will develop the plans and superintend the processes of healing every scar produced by sin. Repentant Christians can be assured of His personal interest, which will lead to a fulfilling relationship with God, with others, and with themselves. He sincerely wants all believers to achieve wholeness in every area of their lives.

---

[166] Gordon McDonald, Rebuilding Your Broken World (Nashville: Oliver-Nelson Books, 1988), 184.

The Holy Spirit will lead those who wish to repent from sins to those Spirit-filled people with whom they can trust the most personal areas of their lives.

All Christians are also potential members of these support networks. The Bible commands believers to support those who are weak (Acts 20:35 and 1 Thessalonians 5:14). They should be willing to embrace those who are ασθενης: "weak, infirm, feeble, without strength."[167] They need to stand emotionally and spiritually beside others who are in need.

The only Christians, however, who qualify to help other believers are those who

---

[167] Friedrich, <u>Theological Dictionary of the New Testament</u>, vol. 1, 490.

meet the prerequisite of being controlled by the Holy Spirit. Paul, in Ephesians 5:18, commands all believers to be filled with the Holy Spirit. The command to be filled, or πληρουσθε, means "to render full, to complete, to fill to the top so that nothing shall be wanting to full measure, to fill to the brim."[168]   This filling occurs when believers voluntarily allow the Holy Spirit to take the complete oversight of their thought lives and actions.   These Spirit-filled believers can help the Lord in the restoration of others.

---

[168]   Friedrich, <u>Theological Dictionary of the New Testament</u>, vol. 6, 286.

A MODEL FOR COUNSELING

The Bible is replete with principles to guide relationships within the church. The model for church discipline is one such example.

A Progression in Counseling

PRIVATE SETTING

The Bible teaches a progression in pastoral counseling illustrated by church discipline. Jesus says in Matthew 18:15-17:

> *Moreover if thy brother shall trespass against thee, go and tell him his fault between thee and him alone: if he shall hear thee, thou hast gained thy brother. But if he will not hear thee, then take with thee one or two more, that in the mouth of two or three witnesses every word may be established. And if he shall neglect to hear them, tell it unto the church: but if he neglect to hear the church, let him be unto thee as an heathen man and a publican.*

Counseling, according to verse 15, should begin individually. The counselor and counselee should be the only ones involved. Confidentiality, a crucial element of counseling, is implied. Thomas F. Taylor, executive director of the Institute for Ministry, Law, and Ethics states: "Maintaining a high respect for privacy is crucial to all ministries."[169]

---

[169] Thomas F. Taylor, "Will Your Church be Sued?," Christianity Today, January 6, 1997, 42.

Jeff Noblit asserted, "A private sin receives a private rebuke."[170] A responsive counselee need not be confronted on a large scale when they willing to respond on a small scale.

SMALL GROUP SETTING

Personal counseling, when rejected, progresses to a small group setting. According to conciliator Ken Sande, "If repeated efforts to resolve the matter through private discussions fail, and if the matter is too serious to over-look, you may then ask one or more people to

---

[170] Noblit, "The Principle of Church Discipline," audiotape.

intervene."[171] Two or three additional people are included (verse 16) to encourage the counselee to conform to biblical admonitions; the element of confidentiality, however, is still maintained (though less than in an individual setting).

Others may become involved in two ways. This can occur either by mutual agreement or by one's own initiative.[172] The first means, mutual agreement, is usually more beneficial. Adams states that:

> *Solutions to difficulties are often reached much more permanently, much more effectively, and*

---

[171] Ken Sande, The Peacemaker (Grand Rapids: Baker Book House, 1991), 146.

[172] Sande, The Peacemaker, 147-148.

> *much more rapidly when all the parties of a*
> *controversy are included in counseling.*[173]

The other members of the problem or dispute are invited to participate in seeking a solution, and to aid the counselee in moving toward wholeness.

A second means of involving others, one's own initiative, becomes necessary when the counselee rejects the suggestion of outside involvement. Sande substitutes the word opponent for the word counselee in the following statement: "While mutual agreement is always preferable, it is not actually required if your opponent professes to be a Christian."[174]

---

[173] Jay E. Adams, Competent to Counsel (Grand Rapids: Zondervan Publishing House, 1970), 237.

[174] Sande, The Peacemaker, 148.

Pastoral counselors are working within sound Biblical constraints, therefore, when they approach a counselee in this manner.

A qualification, however, is that counselors should notify counselees of their intentions. Sande continued: "it is wise and often beneficial to warn your opponent of what you are about to do."[175] Counselees should have the opportunity to either repent or properly prepare for the meeting.

LARGE GROUP SETTING

The process continues to a larger group setting. The church becomes involved (verse

---

[175] Sande, <u>The Peacemaker</u>, 148.

17). A degree of confidentiality should still be maintained. Sande stated:

> *This does not mean standing up in a worship service and broadcasting the conflict to church members and visitors alike, since unwarranted publicity is totally inconsistent with the tenor of Matthew 18. Instead, you should inform the leadership of the other person's church (and probably yours as well) of the problem, and, pursuant to 1 Corinthians 6:1-8, request their assistance in resolving the matter.*[176]

Noblit's position was in agreeement with Sande's statement: "Now in a church our size, that doesn't necessarily mean the whole

---

[176] Sande, The Peacemaker, 151.

congregation. It may mean the Sunday school class."[177] He further stated:

> *It means tell a group of people so that a group of people can be praying that that person would repent. And a group of people can go after them. And a group of people can knock on their door, and say that we love you. We love you, but this can't go on—you've got to get this right.*

The purpose at this level is twofold: to attempt to restore the person using a high degree of accountability, and to clarify the church's position regarding the sin. First, this level presents the counselee with a tremendous amount of accountability. The entire church is

---

[177] Noblit, "The Principle of Church Discipline," audiotape.

expressing the opinion that the counselee's activities are unbiblical, and must be changed.

Second, the church is clarifying its position regarding the sin. The counselee is not the only one who is in jeopardy; all church members have the potential for committing the same sin. They must, therefore, observe the consequences associated with a life of disobedience to God's Word.

Exclusion from the Group

A counselee who continually refuses to conform to biblical teachings must, ultimately, be treated "as an heathen man and a publican" (Matt. 18:17). This means that "if a person behaves like a nonbeliever would—namely, by disregarding the authority of Scripture and of Christ's church—he is to be treated as a nonbeliever."[178] Jeff Noblit said, "Consider him an outsider—outside the local church family; remove him from church membership."[179]

Treating others as outsiders does not mean to neglect them. Unrepentant counselees should be evangelized as unbelievers. The ultimate goal for them is restoration to the Lord.

They should, however, be kept from participation in the membership functions of the church. Sande also believes that, in extreme

---

[178] Sande, <u>The Peacemaker</u>, 152.

[179] Noblit, "The Principle of Church Discipline," audiotape.

cases, "if the person is behaving in a way that disrupts the peace of the church, it may also be appropriate to exclude him or her from church property."[180]

RESPONSES TO CHURCH DISCIPLINE

ACCEPTANCE

People respond to church discipline in one of three basic ways. First, some church members are extremely responsive to correction, and want to know the truth. They

---

[180] Sande, <u>The Peacemaker</u>, 152.

will change their behavior to conform to God's principles. These Christians, consisting primarily of new believers, have never clearly understood the Biblical teachings regarding their conduct. They are ignorant of the facts; they are willing to obey once they become informed.

RESISTANCE

Another response to discipline is resistance to change. This includes those church members who are described in Acts 28:27:

> *For the heart of this people is waxed gross, and their ears are dull of hearing, and their eyes have they closed; lest they should see with their eyes, and hear with their ears, and understand*

*with their heart, and should be converted, and
I should heal them.*

These church members refuse to believe their activities may be classified as sin. They constantly reject the public teachings of the Bible in a public setting regarding their lifestyles, but are more likely to respond in a private, personal conversation. They need the confrontation of a Christian sharing God's Word with them individually in order to produce repentance.

REJECTION

A third response is total rejection of both preaching and private confrontation. This category is made up of those who choose to live in open defiance to the clear principles of God's

Word. They know what the Bible teaches; they prefer to totally disregard its instruction. These people may require additional steps, including bringing in witnesses, public confrontation of their behavior, and disclosure of their behavior before the church. They may ultimately require expulsion from the group of believers.

PROBLEMS ASSOCIATED WITH CHURCH DISCIPLINE

Church discipline is a category of counseling which has been overlooked by many pastors in recent years. They have avoided this field of correction for several reasons.

TEMPORARILY DISRUPTIVE

One reason is that church discipline can be temporarily disruptive in the life of a church. An element of conflict within the group invariably arises as sin is confronted.

"Destructive controversy has a tendency to expand."[181] It starts at the individual level, and may progress to a group level as the one being confronted enlists support from family and friends within the church.

---

[181] Robert Bolton, <u>People Skills</u> (New York: Simon and Schuster, 1979), 206.

NEED FOR PERSONAL ACCEPTANCE

A second reason for avoidance is that pastors cannot adequately minister in a hostile environment. They believe they need a degree of acceptance from their church members.

Pastors face potential rejection as they seek to deal in disciplinary matters. Some people with whom they minister have not historically been responsive to scriptural solutions to their problems. These people believe they can personally solve their problems without God's intervention.

Those members who reject the scriptures will also likely reject pastors who offer Bible-based counsel. They may even act with open malevolence toward those ministers. Pastors must not allow themselves to avoid the disciplinary process in an effort to temporarily preserve harmony in the church and appease these church members. They must attempt to help the members despite their unwillingness to be restored.

PERSONAL INADEQUACY

A third reason for pastoral aversion is a sense of personal inadequacy. Pastors may feel they have not been sufficiently trained to deal directly with the sins of church members. This frequently occurs because "not enough thought is given to the future pastor's ability to enter wisely and deeply into people's lives with the truth he believes."[182]

Pastors may also have personal sin problems that, they feel, make them unworthy to confront the sins of others. They are intimidated by a misunderstanding of Jesus' teachings in Luke 6:41-42:

> *And why beholdest thou the mote that is in thy brother's eye, but perceivest not the beam that is in thine own eye? Either how canst thou say to thy brother, "Brother, let me pull out the mote that is in thine eye," when thou thyself beholdest not the beam that is in thine own eye? Thou hypocrite, cast out first the beam out of thine own eye, and then shalt thou see clearly to pull out the mote that is in thy brother's eye.*

---

[182] Larry Crabb, Understanding People (Grand Rapids: Zondervan Publishing House, 1987), 66.

Pastors are to deal with their own sin problems in order to help others. They should not, therefore, avoid confrontations in an effort to hide their own inadequacies.

They may, in addition, simply be unwilling to participate in personal meetings of any kind. They find themselves too busy with administrative matters or their public ministries to spend time individually with church members.

These pastors must focus on the teachings of Acts 2:46-47:

> *And they, continuing daily with one accord in the temple, and breaking bread from house to house, did eat their meat with gladness and singleness of heart, praising God, and having favour with all the people. And the Lord added to the church daily such as should be saved.*

The Lord blesses both the corporate and the private aspects of the ministry. Both are essential for properly equipping and correcting church members.

INTRUSIVE NATURE

A fourth reason is that discipline is, by nature, intrusive. Intrusive means: "characterized by intrusion, intruding where one is not welcome or invited."[183] Most frequently the pastor becomes informed of the need through a third party, and must initiate the meeting.

---

[183] <u>Merriam-Webster's Collegiate Dictionary</u>, 10th edition, 615.

Conflict, however, should not be avoided, but "viewed as a normal, in fact, inevitable, slice of life."[184] Discipline, when exercised properly, will ultimately diminish any conflicts it seems to create in the church.

FEAR OF LITIGATION

A fifth reason pastors may fear the process of church discipline is the potential for litigation. This fear is not totally unfounded, as today's church is a definite target for legal action. Thomas F. Taylor stated:

---

[184] David G. Benner, ed. <u>Baker Encyclopedia of Psychology</u> (Grand Rapids: Baker Book House, 1985), 215.

What is a minister's worst nightmare? How about a large group of lawyers gathered together to discuss the best way to sue clergy and churches? In 1992 the American Bar Association hosted just such a seminar, and similar ones have been held regionally across the country since then. What is disturbing about these meetings is not their intention of bringing those clergy or churches that act illegally to justice—wrongdoers should be held responsible—but their emphasis oftentimes on how to land large settlement amounts.[185]

This fear, however, should not keep pastors from obeying the Biblical admonition to exercise needed discipline. They must realize that the church belongs to God, and must be operated as He prescribes. Noblit asserted:

---

[185] Taylor, "Will Your Church be Sued?," 42.

And we're here not to do what we think, doesn't matter what the majority rules of the majority votes or what the committee says, and what the board of deacons decides; if they violate what the owner says, they're wrong. He owns it.[186]

FEAR OF BEING SCRUTINIZED PERSONALLY

A sixth reason is a fear of being scrutinized personally. Many pastors do not want their own lives inspected, and so remain distant from their church members. They seek a mutual laissez-faire situation.

Samuel, in contrast, invited scrutiny. 1 Samuel 12:1-3 says:

---

[186] Noblit, "The Principle of Church Discipline," audiotape.

> *And Samuel said unto all Israel, Behold, I have hearkened unto your voice in all that ye said unto me, and have made a king over you. And now, behold, the king walketh before you: and I am old and grayheaded; and, behold, my sons are with you: and I have walked before you from my childhood unto this day. Behold, here I am: witness against me before the LORD, and before his anointed: whose ox have I taken? or whose ass have I taken? or whom have I defrauded? whom have I oppressed? or of whose hand have I received any bribe to blind mine eyes therewith? and I will restore it you. He allowed, in essence, anyone in the entire nation to speak against him. His confidence, based upon his faithfulness in serving the Lord, was unwavering.*

The Apostle Paul also invited scrutiny of his life in 1 Corinthians 11:1: "Be ye followers of me, even as I also am of Christ." He told them that, by observing his life, they would be observing the actions of Jesus.

All pastors, to effectively work with others, need to imitate the examples set by Samuel and the Apostle Paul. They ought to allow others the opportunity to investigate their lives and ministries. This openness to examination will be reflected in the lives of their church members, and produce a healthy environment for church discipline.

GUIDELINES FOR CHURCH DISCIPLINE

Certain guidelines should be applied when using church discipline. The following stipulations will both alleviate the fears pastors may have and prevent the process from being misused.

REDEMPTIVE

First, discipline must be done redemptively. The New Testament word for redemption is απολυτρωσις, and means: "a releasing effected by payment of ransom."[187] The purpose of church discipline, then, should be to liberate believers from the ongoing relational consequences of their sins.

The most serious relational consequence is broken fellowship with God. Discipline should seek to restore fallen believers to healthy relationships with God.

A restored relationship with God will

---

[187] Friedrich, <u>Theological Dictionary of the New Testament</u>, vol. 4, 351.

result in a right relationship with others. The converse of 1 John 4:20 is true: "If a man say, I love God, and hateth his brother, he is a liar: for he that loveth not his brother whom he hath seen, how can he love God whom he hath not seen." Believers who are restored in their fellowship with God are fully equipped to be in right relationships with others.

IMMEDIATE

Church discipline must also be practiced immediately. Pastors must address the problem when they are made aware of its presence. The Bible teaches in Numbers 30:3-5 that:

> *If a woman also vow a vow unto the Lord, and bind herself by a bond, being in her father's house in her youth; and her father hear her vow, and her bond wherewith she hath bound*

> *her soul, and her father shall hold his peace at her: then all her vows shall stand, and every bond wherewith she hath bound her soul shall stand. But if her father disallow her in the day that he heareth: not any of her vows, or of her bonds wherewith she hath bound her soul, shall stand: and the Lord shall forgive her, because her father disallowed her.*

This timeliness is crucial for two reasons. First, the seriousness with which a confirmed sin is perceived diminishes with time. An active sin that is overlooked for any reason cannot be dealt with effectively after a significant period has elapsed.

Second, promptness is important in discovering the false accusation of sin. Christians who are innocent need to be vindicated by the pastor and their accusers.

IMPARTIAL

Church discipline should be done impartially. Pastors tend to address sin in the lives of those people they consider to be "expendable" while overlooking sin in the lives of "prominent" people. James 2 refers to the problem of having a "respect of persons," or προσοπολεπσια. Προσοπολεπσια may be defined as:

> *the fault of one who when called on to give judgment has respect of the outward circumstances of man and not to their intrinsic merits, and so prefers, as the more worthy, one who is rich, high born, or powerful, to another who does not have these qualities.*[188]

---

[188] Friedrich, <u>Theological Dictionary of the New Testament</u>, vol. 6, 950.

All Christians should be treated with the same dignity as those who are wealthy, have influential positions, or are notable in the community. There can be no extenuating factors if discipline is to be carried out effectively.

CONCLUSION

Church discipline is an essential element of the healthy church. Pastors must be willing to exercise it if local churches are to survive.

First, discipline must be practiced to be obedient to God. Church discipline is the means God has chosen in dealing with the rejection of His leadership in people's lives.

Second, sin cannot be adequately addressed from the pulpit. Pastors must be willing to meet with church members privately to properly apply the Bible to their specific needs within the church.

Third, sin must be addressed because of its ability to damage the lives of individual church members. Sin destroys the testimonies of Christians as it weakens their relationships with the Lord.

Fourth, it must be confronted before it affects the corporate body of believers. Sin that is not confronted can gain approval in the church. Christians who overlook sin eventually accept it, and assimilate it into their lives. Sin that could have been contained begins to spread its way throughout the church, and inevitably destroys the effectiveness of the congregation in the community.

Church discipline is, therefore, an integral part of pastoral counseling. Pastors will find it to be an extremely useful tool in the effective leadership of their churches.

BIBLIOGRAPHY

BOOKS

Adams, Jay E. Competent to Counsel. Grand Rapids: Zondervan Publishing House, 1970.

Barna, Charles. User Friendly Churches: What Christians Need to Know About the Churches People Love to Go To. Ventura, CA: Regal Books, 1991.

Benner, David G., ed. Baker Encyclopedia of Psychology. Grand Rapids: Baker Book House, 1985.

Biehl, Bobb. Stop Setting Goals If You Would Rather Solve Problems. Nashville: Moorings, Random House, Inc., 1995.

Bolton, Robert. People Skills. New York: Simon
and Schuster, 1979.

Bowman, Ray and Eddy Hall. When Not to
Build: An Architect's Unconventional
Wisdom for the Growing Church. Grand
Rapids: Baker Book House, 1992.

Bruce, F. F. Commentary on the Book of the
Acts. In The New International
Commentary on the New Testament. F.
F. Bruce, gen. ed. Grand Rapids: Wm. B.
Eerdmans Publishing Co., 1976.

Brunnen-Verlag, Giessen. A Linguistic Key to
the Greek NewTestament, Trans. Fritz
Rienecker. Ed. Cleon L. Rogers,Jr.
Grand Rapids: Zondervan Publishing
House, 1980.

Bryson, Harold T. Expository Preaching.
Nashville: Broadman And Holman
Publishers, 1995.

Buchsel, F. "Apolutrosis." In <u>Theological Dictionary of the New Testament</u>. Vol. 4. Edited by Gerhard Friedrich, 335-356. Grand Rapids: Wm. B. Eerdmans Publishing House, 1974.

Buford, Bob. Interview by Jim Roberts (9 April 1991). Quoted in Chuck Colson and Jack Eckerd. <u>Why America Doesn't Work</u>. Dallas, TX: Word Publishing, 1991.

Bultman, R. "Eulabes." In <u>Theological Dictionary of the NewTestament</u>. Vol. 2. Ed. Gerhard Friedrich. Grand Rapids: Wm. B. Eerdmans Publishing Co., 1974.

Callahan, Kennon L. <u>Twelve Keys to an Effective Church: Strategic Planning for Mission</u>. San Francisco, CA: HarperSanFrancisco, Harper Collins Publishers, 1983.

Carter, Les and Jim Underwood. <u>The Significance Principle: The Secret Behind High Performance People and Organizations</u>. Nashville: Broadman and Holman Publishers, 1998.

Crabb, Larry. Understanding People. Grand
    Rapids: Zondevan Publishing House,
    1987.

Davis, Ron Lee. Mistreated. Portland, OR:
    Multnomah Press, 1989.

Delling, G. "Pleroma." In Theological Dictionary
    of the New Testament. Vol. 6. Edited by
    Gerhard Friedrich, 283-311. Grand
    Rapids: Wm. B. Eerdmans Publishing
    House, 1974.

Dewey, John C. Human Nature and Conduct.
    New York: Modern Library, 1930). In
    Robert Bolton, People Skills. New York:
    Simon and Schuster, Inc., 1979; reprint,
    New York: Touchstone Books, 1986.

Ellenburg, Dale. "Doctor of Ministry Seminar:
    Interpretation/Preaching." Notebook of
    materials from a seminar   sponsored by
    Mid-America Baptist Theological
    Seminary. Memphis, TN. 28 October,
    1997, photocopied.

Erickson, Millard J. and James L. Heflin. <u>Old Wine in New Wineskins</u>.Grand Rapids: Baker Book House Co., 1997.

Fee, Gordon D. and Douglas Stewart. <u>How to Read the Biblefor All Its Worth</u>. Grand Rapids: Zondervan Publishing House, 1993.

Fields, Doug. <u>Purpose Driven Youth Ministry: Nine Essential Foundations for Healthy Growth</u>. Grand Rapids: Zondervan Publishing House, 1998.

<u>Funk and Wagnall's Encyclopedia</u>, 1998 ed. S.v. "Henry Ford."

Grimm, [Carl Ludwig], and [Christian Gottlob] Wilke. <u>Greek-English Lexicon of the New Testament</u>. Translated and revised by Joseph Henry Thayer. New York: American Book Co., 1889; reprint, Grand Rapids: Zondervan Publishing House, 1981).

Gallagher, Steve. Tearing Down the High Places
of Sexual Idolatry. Crittendon, KY: Pure
Life Press, 1986.

Greidanus, Sidney. The Modern Preacher and
the Ancient Text. Grand Rapids: Wm. B.
Eerdmans Publishing Co., 1988.

Harris, R. Laird, Gleason L. Archer, and Bruce
R. Waltke, eds. Theological Wordbook of
the Old Testament. Vol. A. Chicago:
Moody Press, 1980.

Hemfelt, Robert, Frank Minirth, and Paul
Meier. Love is a Choice. Nashville:
Thomas Nelson Publishers, 1989.

Johnson, Laney L. The Church: God's People
on Mission. Nashville: Convention Press,
1995.

Kaiser, Walter C. Toward an Exegetical
Theology. Grand Rapids: Baker Book
House Co., 1981.

Lord, Peter. Hearing God. Grand Rapids:
Baker Book House Co., 1988.

Lohse, E. "Prosolempsia." In <u>Theological Dictionary of the New Testament</u>. Vol. 6. Edited by Gerhard Friedrich, 768-780. Grand Rapids: Wm. B. Eerdmans Publishing House, 1974.

Maxwell, John C. <u>Developing the Leaders Around You: How to Help Others Reach Their Full Potential</u>. Nashville: Thomas Nelson Publishers, 1995.

Maxwell, John C. <u>Ushers and Greeters</u>. El Cajon, CA: INJOY Ministries, 1991 quoted in Gary L. McIntosh. <u>The Exodus Principle: A Five-Part Strategy to Free Your People For Ministry</u>. Nashville: Broadman and Holman Publishers, 1995.

McDonald, Gordon. <u>Rebuilding Your Broken World</u>. Nashville: Oliver-Nelson Books, 1988.

McIntosh, Gary L. <u>The Exodus Principle: A Five-Part Strategyt to Free Your People for Ministry</u>. Nashville: Broadman and Holman Publishers, 1995.

McGee, Robert S. The Search for Significance.
        Nashville: Lifeway Press, 1992. Merriam
        Webster's Collegiate Dictionary, 10th
        Edition. Springfield, MA: Merriam-
        Webster, Inc., 1995.

Merriam Webster's Collegiate Dictionary, 10th
        Edition. Springfield, MA: Merriam-
        Webster, Inc., 1995.

Microsoft Encarta Encyclopedia, 1999 ed. S.v.
        "Assembly Line."

Moore, W. Scott. Partners in Planting: Starting
        and Staffing a New Testament Church.
        Rogersville, AL: Eleos Press, 2012.

Miller, James B. The Corporate Coach. New
        York: St. Martin's Press, 1993.

Odiam, Alan. "Doctor of Ministry Seminar:
        Interpretation/Preaching." Notebook of
        materials from a seminar sponsored by
        Mid-America Baptist Theological
        Seminary. Memphis, TN. 28 October,
        1997, photocopied.

Phillips, John. Acts 13-28. Vol. 2. In Exploring Acts. Chicago, IL: Moody Press, 1986.

Professional Sales Development—Phase I: You and Your Family. U.S.A.: Metropolitan Life Insurance Company, 1976.

Rainer, Thom. Effective Evangelistic Churches. Nashville: Broadman and Holman Publishers, 1996.

Sande, Ken. The Peacemaker. Grand Rapids: Baker Book House, 1991.

Schneider, J. "Time." In Theological Dictionary of the New Testament. Vol. 8. Edited by Gerhard Friedrich, 169-180. Grand Rapids: Wm. B. Eerdmans Publishing House, 1974.

Schrenk, G. "Eulabes." In Theological Dictionary of the NewTestament. Vol. 5. Ed. Gerhard Friedrich. Grand Rapids: Wm. B. Eerdmans Publishing Co., 1974.

Seamands, David A. Living With Your Dreams.
Wheaton, IL: Victor Books, 1990.

Smith, J. B. Greek-English Concordance to the
New Testament, A Tabular and Statistical
Greek-English Concordance Based on
the King James Version with an English-
to-Greek Index. Scottsdale, PA: Herald
Press, 1955.

Stahlin, G. "Asthenes." In Theological Dictionary
of the New Testament. Vol. 1. Edited by
Gerhard Friedrich, 491-493. Grand
Rapids: Wm. B. Eerdmans Publishing
House, 1974.

Stauffer, E. "Epitimao." In Theological
Dictionary of the New Testament. Vol. 2.
Edited by Gerhard Friedrich, 623-627.
Grand Rapids: Wm. B. Eerdmans
Publishing House, 1974.

Strathmann, H. "Martyreo." In <u>Theological Dictionary of the New Testament</u>. Vol. 4. Ed. Gerhard Friedrich. Grand Rapids: Wm. B. Eerdmans Publishing Co., 1974.

<u>Theological Dictionary of the New Testament</u>. 6 vols. Ed. Gerhard Friedrich. Grand Rapids: Wm. B. Eerdmans Publishing Co., 1974.

Thomas, Robert L. "Exegesis and Expository Preaching." In <u>Rediscovering Expository Preaching</u>. Ed. Richard L. Mayhue. Dallas, TX: Word Publishing Co., 1992.

Torrey, R. A. <u>The Power of Prayer</u>. Grand Rapids: Zondervan Publishing Co., 1971.

Toussaint, Stanley D. "Acts." In <u>Bible Knowledge Commentary</u>. New Testament edition. Eds. John V. Walvoord and Roy B. Zuck. Wheaton, IL: Victor Books, 1983.

United Bible Societies. <u>The Greek New Testament</u>. 3d ed. New York: American Bible Society, 1975.

Vincent, Marvin R. Word Studies in the New Testament. 3 vols. Grand Rapids: Wm. B. Eerdmans Publishing Co., 1989.

Von Soden, H. "Adelphos." In Theological Dictionary of the New Testament. Vol. 1. Ed. Gerhard Friedrich. Grand Rapids: Wm. B. Eerdmans Publishing Co., 1974.

Wagner, C. Peter. Leading Your Church to Growth: The Secret of Pastor/People Partnership in Dynamic Church Growth. Ventura, CA: Regal Books, 1984.

Wagner, C. Peter and Richard L. Gorsuch. "The Quality Church (Part 1)." Leadership Winter 1983, 31. Quoted in John N. Vaughan. The Large Church: A Twentieth-Century Expression of the First-Century Church. Grand Rapids: Baker Book House, 1985.

Warren, Rick. The Purpose Driven Church: Growth without Compromising Your Message and Mission. Grand Rapids: Zondervan Publishing House, 1995.

Wiersbe, Warren W. <u>Wiersbe's Expository Outlines on the New Testament</u>. Wheaton, IL: Victor Books, 1992.

White, James Emery. <u>Opening the Front Door: Worship and Church Growth</u>. Nashville: Convention Press, 1992.

<u>World Book Encyclopedia</u>, 1985 ed. S.v. "Assembly Line."

<u>World Book Encyclopedia</u>, 1985 ed. S.v. Automation."
<u>World Book Encyclopedia</u>, 1985 ed. S.v. "Automobile."

Ziglar, Zig. <u>See You At the Top</u>. Gretna, LA: Pelican Publishing Company, 1975.

AUDIOTAPES

Noblit, Jeff. <u>The Principle of Church Discipline</u>. Audiotape of a sermon presented at First Baptist Church, Muscle Shoals, AL, 1997.

NEWSPAPERS

"Effective Churches: Barna Reveals Church Habits Necessary for Greater Effectiveness in Ministry." <u>The Alabama Baptist</u>. 7 May 1998.

Jenkins, Edwin F. "The Altitude of Church Growth: An Issue of Attitude or Aptitude?" <u>The Alabama Baptist</u>. 30 April 1998.

PERIODICALS

Taylor, Thomas F. "Will Your Church be Sued?" <u>Christianity Today</u>. (January 6, 1997): 41-48.

UNPUBLISHED MATERIALS

Moore, W. Scott. "Multiple Morning Worship Service Questionnaire." Moulton, AL: Pleasant Grove Baptist Church, 1998.

W. Scott Moore

During a ministerial career of more than three decades, Christian author W. Scott Moore, Bachelor of Business Administration, Master of Divinity, Doctor of Ministry, has served as bus minister, children's pastor, youth minister, and associate pastor. He is currently the senior pastor of a rural church in north Alabama.